*The
Impact
of
Alcoholism*

THE IMPACT OF ALCOHOLISM

by Steven F. Bucky, Ph.D.

and

Richard Boyatzis, Ph.D.
Jere Bunn
Barbara Czescik, M.A.
Anthony Del Nuovo, M.A.
Gloria Gray, Ph.D.
Douglas Harry, LL.B.
David Jacobs, Ph.D.
Rosalie Jesse, Ph.D.
James Massman, M.D.
Adrienne McFadd, Ph.D.

HAZELDEN/
CENTER CITY, MN 55012

1978

First published, May, 1978

80-1103

Copyright © 1978 by Steven F. Bucky, Ph.D.
All rights reserved
No part of this book may be reproduced
in any form without the written
permission of the publisher.

  ISBN: 0-89486-044-5

  Library of Congress Card Catalog Number: 78-52647

Printed in the United States of America

To
CLANCY and JEANNE . . .
two of my favorite alcoholics

Table of Contents

I. Signs and Symptoms
   Steven F. Bucky, Ph.D. 1

II. Medical Aspects of Alcoholism
   *James Massman, M.D., and
   Steven F. Bucky, Ph.D.* 11

III. Personal and Emotional Aspects of Alcoholism
   Steven F. Bucky, Ph.D. 27

IV. Legal Aspects of Alcoholism
   *Douglas Harry, LL.B., and
   Steven F. Bucky, Ph.D.* 35

V. Interpersonal Effects of Alcohol Abuse
   *Rosalie Jesse, Ph.D., Adrienne McFadd, Ph.D.,
   Gloria Gray, Ph.D., and Steven F. Bucky,
   Ph.D.* 45

VI. Effects of Alcohol Abuse on Work Performance
   Steven F. Bucky, Ph.D. 69

VII. Treatment
   Steven F. Bucky, Ph.D., et. al. 75

VIII. Attitude and Behavior Changes
   Steven F. Bucky, Ph.D. 113

CHAPTER I

Signs and Symptoms

Steven F. Bucky, Ph.D.

Alcoholism and alcohol abuse have a destructive impact on our society. Recent statistics indicate that there are approximately ninety-five million adult drinkers in the country, and perhaps nine million of them drink to excess. The alcohol abuser injures not only himself, but his family and other concerned persons as well. More than thirty-six million Americans are victims of the insidious and far-reaching effects of the disease, often without recognizing the problem for what it really is.

The illness of alcoholism can strike anyone, but it is most common in the thirty-five to fifty-five age group. The average age of alcoholics is, however, steadily decreasing, and approximately 5 percent of problem drinkers are teen-agers. Although the stereotype of an alcoholic is that of a skid row derelict gulping cheap wine and sleeping on sidewalks, only 3 to 5 percent of the victims of the illness actually fit that description. Many of them are well-dressed and hold good jobs.

Alcoholism is one of the leading health problems in the United States today, and there are many different programs designed to treat it. Because they vary in quality and many different types of alcoholics find their way into treatment, success rates range all the way from 30 to 70 percent. Early intervention is of paramount importance, for the sooner an individual receives treatment, the greater are his chances of winning the battle against the disease.

Alcoholism threatens the very lives of its victims, decreasing the average life span by ten to twelve years and causing eighty-five thousand unnecessary deaths annually. Because the illness progresses so gradually, determining whether an alcohol problem actually exists can be an extremely difficult task. To complicate matters further, many problem drinkers do not experience all of the symptoms of alcoholism. Usually, however, there is a general sequence from what those in the field call early alcoholism, or the Prodromal Stage, to the degeneration of advanced alcoholism, or the Chronic Stage.

Different symptoms reflecting the progressive nature of the disease usually become painfully visible with each succeeding stage of development. The following paragraphs describe these symptoms.

The Pre-alcoholic Stage

In the Pre-alcoholic Stage, a person drinks to reduce tension and anxiety and to avoid conflict. While his pain does disappear temporarily, he must consume more and more alcohol to achieve the euphoric effect he is seeking so desperately. As his drinking increases, he takes the irrevocable step across an imaginary line into what Jellinek calls the Prodromal Stage of alcoholism. The Crucial and Chronic Stages follow.

The Prodromal Stage

During the Prodromal Stage, symptoms of alcoholism become disturbingly apparent. They usually include the following warning signs:

Blackouts

Blackouts are not the result of passing out but are a form of amnesia caused by too much alcohol. The individual simply cannot remember what happened while he was drinking. These blackouts bewilder and distress him, and as he consumes more and more alcohol, they occur with frightening regularity and last longer than they did initially. Recently, a patient reported that he remembered driving out of San Diego, but could recall nothing else until, four days later, he saw a sign saying, "Entering Phoenix, Arizona."

Gulping and Sneaking Drinks

The individual grows more and more dependent upon the pampering effects of alcohol. He no longer sips drinks leisurely but swallows them quickly in a vain effort to achieve the illusory state of happiness he imagines he can find in the bottle. He sneaks extra drinks and finds it is imperative for him to have a few before attending a party or facing a business meeting. He feels guilty and begins to avoid talking about drinking.

Chronic Hangover

Alcohol becomes more and more necessary to protect and cushion the drinker from the buffeting of daily living. "Morning after" discomfort becomes increasingly frequent, resulting in an almost continual state of distress.

Eye-Openers

To alleviate his painful hangovers, the individual begins to need a drink in the morning to "start the day right." The alcohol he consumes also relieves his feelings of guilt, remorse, and depression, and he feels he cannot face the day without this drink.

Preoccupation with Drinking

The individual begins to drink more heavily and more

4 / THE IMPACT OF ALCOHOLISM

often than his friends. Getting drunk becomes a habit, and when he is intoxicated, he may try desperately to feel important, perhaps by throwing his money around or indulging in other conspicuous ways of seeking attention.

Avoiding Reference to Drinking

The mere act of talking about drinking begins to threaten the individual, and when the topic of conversation turns to alcohol, he tries to change the subject or withdraw from the group. Sometimes, on the other hand, he may deal with such discussions by bragging about his drinking exploits or declaring defensively, "This is clearly not a problem for me."

Crucial Stage

Loss of Control

During this phase, the individual loses the ability to stop drinking once he starts. He may have no trouble refusing the first drink, but even a small amount of alcohol is likely to trigger a destructive chain reaction, causing him to drink himself into an intoxicated state. This is one of the primary symptoms of alcoholism.

Alibi System

The individual feels intensely guilty because he cannot control his drinking. He becomes defensive, constructing an elaborate system of reasons for his behavior in a futile attempt to convince family, associates, and most of all, himself, that he has no problem.

Changing the Pattern

Under pressure from family or employer, the drinker makes a tremendous effort to break the hold alcohol has on him. He sets up rules on when or what he will drink. He may go "on the wagon" for a period of time. But a single drink of alcohol may set the fateful chain reaction in motion again.

SIGNS AND SYMPTOMS / 5

Rejection of Family

Spouse and children may plead with the alcoholic to change his behavior, protesting that they love to be with him when he is sober, but he is obnoxious and repulsive when drinking. They insist they cannot go on living under such stressful and difficult conditions.

Loss of Friends

The alcoholic may behave so unpleasantly that friends no longer seek his companionship, and the drinker himself begins to spurn others to avoid potential rejection.

Loss of Job

Heavy drinkers are erratic at work, come in late, and leave early. They are frequently sick, have more accidents, and make more mistakes than others. These flagrantly poor work habits often cause their employers to terminate them, or they may quit their jobs in order to avoid the pain of being fired.

Antisocial Behavior

The alcoholic prefers solitary drinking, or he may seek the dubious companionship of other alcoholics. He broods over imagined wrongs and believes that people are staring at or talking about him. He is highly critical of others. Destructiveness or violence may cause additional problems during his drinking episodes, or he may simply fall asleep. At this stage, the spouse comments frequently that when the alcoholic drinks, "he becomes explosive with me or the kids," or "he becomes passive and drowses off." Alcohol abuse causes the drinker to have serious difficulty in relating to his spouse emotionally and sexually.

Geographic Escape

Repeated and painful failures in his relationships with friends, relatives, and supervisors create a desperate need in the alcoholic to flee from his problems. At this stage, he may move to another city or change jobs in an attempt to begin life anew.

Seeks Medical Help

Uncontrolled drinking takes its toll on the alcoholic in the form of progressive physical and mental deterioration. He makes the rounds of hospitals, doctors, and psychologists in a frantic quest for help. Seldom does he receive lasting benefits from his search because he refuses to cooperate or admit the extent of his drinking.

Chronic Stage

When the alcoholic reaches the stage of chronic alcoholism, he loses completely the freedom to decide whether or not to take the first drink. Until this point, he was able to choose to drink or abstain, losing control only after actually consuming alcohol. Now there is a frightening change. His entire existence revolves around getting and consuming alcohol. Drinking has become an obsession, and he must do it whenever and however he can. The symptoms of chronic alcoholism include:

Benders

The alcoholic drinks for days at a time and gets blindly and helplessly drunk. He is completely preoccupied with himself and utterly disregards everything around him, including family, job, and even food and shelter. These destructive, periodic escapes into oblivion mark the beginning of the vicious circle of the final, deadly phase of alcoholism. The victim drinks to escape the very problems that drinking creates.

Tremors

The alcoholic develops the "shakes," a serious nervous condition. After these attacks, he swears off drinking but cannot fight the compulsive urge to return to alcohol for any length

SIGNS AND SYMPTOMS / 7

of time. Delirium tremens, vitamin deficiency, and other serious problems begin to plague him during this period.

Protecting the Supply

His supply of liquor becomes his most treasured possession, and having it available constantly is the most important aspect of his life. He will do or sell anything to obtain alcohol, regardless of the cost or injury to himself or others. He craftily hides his bottles for future use, thus ensuring that he will have a ready reserve to satisfy his continual and obsessive needs. Bottles of alcohol may turn up in toilet bowls or dresser drawers, among underwear, or in inconspicuous places in his office, such as filing cabinets or desk drawers.

Unreasonable Resentments

He shows flagrant hostility toward others. They pose a threat to his precious liquor supply as well as provide a target for him as he turns outward an unconscious desire to punish himself. Unpredictable and frequent outbursts are common, aimed at anyone who happens to be in his way.

Nameless Fears and Anxieties

The alcoholic constantly fears some nebulous, indefinable threat. He suffers from a sense of impending doom and destruction. Nervousness and shakiness plague him, and he is unable to face life without the support of alcohol.

Collapse of the Alibi System

Finally, all of his excuses fail dismally, and he finds he can no longer blame others for his condition. He admits to himself that alcohol has triumphed, and he no longer has any control over it. (This may happen even during earlier stages, in which case the process may repeat itself.)

Surrender Process

If the alcoholic is to recover at this stage, he must totally relinquish the idea of ever drinking again and be willing to seek and accept help. It is imperative that his surrender take place in conjunction with the collapse of the alibi system. Only when the two occur together is there real hope for lasting recovery.

Other Common Terms

The alcoholism community commonly uses several other terms to describe alcoholics and the illness which affects them. E. M. Jellinek defines the different types of alcoholism as follows:

Alpha Alcoholism

Psychological dependency upon alcohol to relieve tension and emotional pain characterizes Alpha Alcoholism.

Beta Alcoholism

Physical disturbances such as cirrhosis and polyneuritis are symptoms of Beta Alcoholism. The victim is so dependent on alcohol that he suffers from withdrawal when he stops drinking.

Gamma Alcoholism

In Gamma Alcoholism, the body develops a tolerance for alcohol. The victim needs more and more of the drug to achieve the euphoric effect he desires. An actual physical dependence on alcohol develops, resulting in such symptoms as the shakes, cold sweats, and preoccupation with drinking. Beta and Gamma Alcoholism have much in common, but the Gamma form involves a greater loss of control, and withdrawal symptoms are more common, frequent, and intense.

Epsilon Alcoholism

Periodic or episodic drinkers may be victims of Epsilon Alcoholism. They may go for long periods of time without drinking too much or getting drunk, but inevitably, there will come a time when the urge for alcohol overcomes them, and they become lost for days in the depths of the bottle.[1]

Assessing an Alcohol Problem

When does a person become a "problem drinker?" At what point does he cross the fateful line from social drinking to alcoholism? Cahalan bases his answers to these questions on the frequency with which a person drinks and the alcohol-related interpersonal, legal, and medical problems that disrupt his life. Data from eleven categories help to determine whether an alcohol problem exists:

1. Frequency of intoxication
2. Binge drinking (drinking for more than one day at a time)
3. Systematic drinking behavior (the inability to stop drinking, sneaking drinks, and similar behavior)
4. Psychological dependence on alcohol
5. Alcohol-related problems with the spouse
6. Alcohol-related problems with friends
7. Alcohol-related problems at work
8. Alcohol-related problems with the law or the police
9. Health problems caused by alcohol
10. Financial problems caused by alcohol
11. Belligerence or fighting associated with alcohol consumption[2]

TABLE 1
SYMPTOMS ASSOCIATED WITH STAGES OF ALCOHOLISM

Pre-alcoholic Stage

Drinking to reduce anxiety

Prodromal Stage

Blackouts
Gulping and sneaking drinks
Chronic hangover
Preoccupation with drinking
Avoiding reference to drinking

Crucial Stage

Loss of control
Alibi system
Eye-openers
Changing the pattern
Rejection of family
Loss of friends
Loss of job
Antisocial behavior
Geographic escape
Seeking medical help

Chronic Stage

Benders
Tremors
Protecting supply
Unreasonable resentments
Nameless fears and anxieties
Collapse of alibi system
Surrender process

CHAPTER II

Medical Aspects of Alcoholism

*James Massman, M.D.,
and Steven F. Bucky, Ph.D.*

Alcohol abuse causes serious and long-lasting damage to the delicate and intricate functionings of the body. When a person falls victim to alcoholism, health and well-being vanish in the depths of the bottle, and life itself may be imperiled. Breaking the ever-tightening grip of an obsessive drinking pattern often results in the painful and dangerous process of withdrawal. The following paragraphs include descriptions of the physical effects of alcohol on the body, intoxicated states, withdrawal syndromes, and a look at Antabuse, a drug used frequently in the treatment of alcoholism.

Physical Damage Resulting from Alcohol Abuse

Alcohol is a powerful toxin to the human body. It threatens virtually every organ system, killing cells and destroying tissues. Alcohol also interferes with the complex metabolism of genetic material and other cells, resulting in a ruinous process that can affect even the unborn.

The popular image of alcohol as a stimulating panacea for depression and anxiety is a fallacious one. Rather, ethyl alcohol depresses the central nervous system, acting upon the brain, spinal cord, and nerves in the same manner as do sedatives, tranquilizers, and general anesthetics.

Excessive drinking causes seriously harmful changes in all human organs. In some individuals, however, there appear to be "target organs," or body systems that, for unknown reasons, suffer more excessively than others from the effects of alcohol abuse. For example, the heart and cardiovascular system may sustain more detrimental effects than other organs in one person, while the liver or pancreas may suffer more in another. Nonetheless, all organ systems undergo severe damage, and the injurious effects of ethyl alcohol upon the body vary drastically according to whether a person is a social drinker, an alcohol abuser, or a hardcore alcoholic.

The Brain

The human brain suffers dramatic and unexpected changes when the body absorbs alcohol. Figure 1 (page 13) illustrates the parts of the brain which undergo the most damage from abuse of the drug.

Small, insidious alterations happen first. The eye, for example, may lose its ability to function normally. Depth perception decreases when the bloodstream contains only a tiny, seemingly harmless amount of alcohol, and there is an increasing loss of peripheral vision as the blood alcohol level increases. Even at low blood alcohol levels, the eye cannot perceive light effectively and fails to respond normally when light energy enters it.

Inhibitions and self-control serve as important guardians of appropriate behavior and personal and community safety. With blood alcohol levels of 0.1 and above, these safeguards rapidly lose their effectiveness. There exists within a person a spurious sense of well-being and false confidence, causing dangerously impaired judgment and an often annoying loquaciousness. Even small doses of alcohol affect the frontal lobe of the brain enough to cause this kind of emotional and behavioral change.

The cerebellum suffers also from small amounts of alcohol. A level of 0.1 can cause a disturbing loss of equilibrium.

FIGURE 1

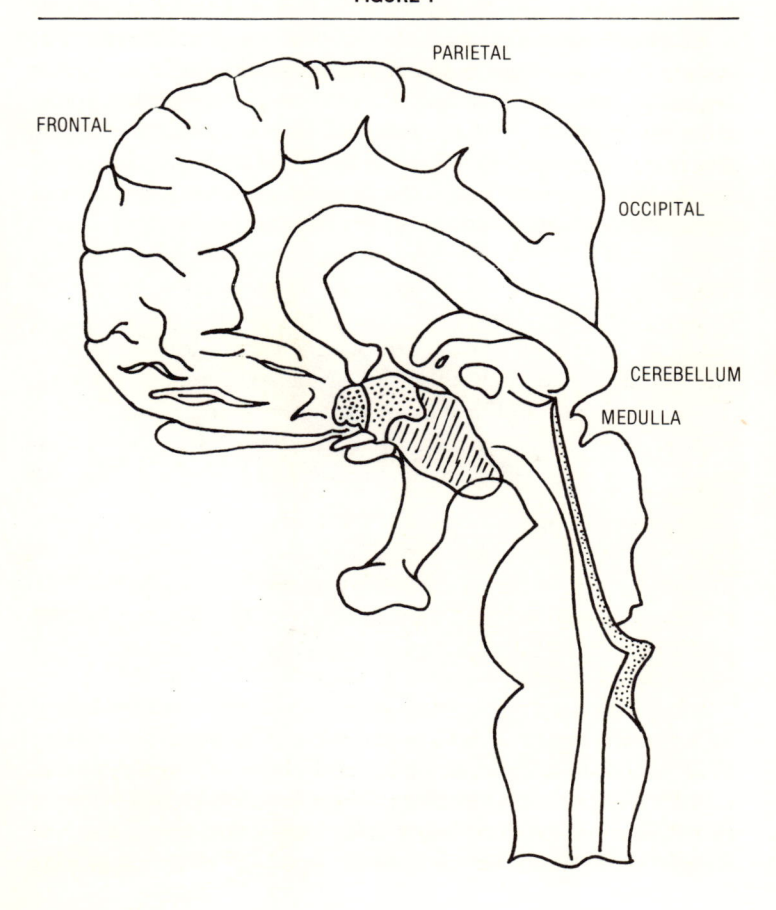

14 / THE IMPACT OF ALCOHOLISM

Consumption which results in a blood alcohol level of 0.2 and above influences the parietal lobe. The drinker suffers a disconcerting loss of control over physical movements, writing and speaking, and other abilities.

When an individual drinks enough to result in a blood alcohol level of 0.2 to 0.3, there is damage to the occipital lobe, causing a decrease in visual skills. A bewildering array of effects plague the drinker, including loss of color perception, distortion, double vision, and loss of depth perception.

Excessive drinking endangers breathing and heart rate, those vital functions which are precious links to life itself. The thalamus and medulla, which control the respiratory and circulatory systems, react to blood alcohol levels of 0.4 and above.

The effects of alcohol on the brain are not always minor or temporary. Heavy drinking may actually destroy brain tissue. In the hardcore drinker, alcohol may so affect the brain that intellect itself suffers considerable impairment. The person may degenerate to such helplessness that he becomes a ward of the state. Some unfortunate individuals destroy enough tissue so that only the brain stem remains active. They deteriorate to the state of being mere vegetables, losing forever the vital essence of their unique selves. Only their respiratory and cardiac centers continue to function. (See the section on Intoxicated States, page 19.)

Bleeding beneath the skull (subdural hematoma) is another consequence of alcoholism. This condition may result in death.

Accidents are common among drinkers, and external injury to the brain, which may cause loss of life, is often the tragic result.

Gastrointestinal System

A person who is drinking experiences a comforting sense of warmth. This deceptive sensation results from the dilation of blood vessels which causes the flow of blood to increase. This process helps the body rid itself of the toxic drug.

The sensitive mucous membranes of the mouth, throat, esophagus, and stomach suffer severe irritation from alcohol, causing a significant increase in the incidence of cancer in these areas. Some researchers claim that the risk of malignancy in the head and neck is as much as fifteen times greater for the heavy drinker than for the nondrinker. Tumors that are the indirect result of alcohol abuse are usually insensitive to x-ray therapy, leaving surgery as the only recourse available. In the nondrinking patient, cancers of the head and neck often respond successfully to x-ray treatment.

Stomach

Most social drinkers, to their chagrin, are well aware of the irritating effects of alcohol on the stomach. They have awakened, perhaps after a party the night before, to "morning after" discomfort in their upper abdomens. They may nurse their hangovers with milk or antacid, and these remedies, together with time, ordinarily relieve their distress.

In heavy drinkers, however, the irritation or inflammation of the stomach may be painfully severe, resulting in gastritis. This condition manifests itself by the symptom of vomiting blood.

Ulcers are a common disorder among drinkers, and they often precede alcoholism. Ironically, the anesthetizing and tranquilizing effects of alcohol may provide welcome relief for the ulcer victim. When the sufferer drinks, alcohol comes into direct contact with the ulcer, reducing the pain. The sedating effects of the drug create a feeling of calmness. This relief is temporary and deceptive, however, for the irritating effects of alcohol are quietly accelerating the ulcer process.

Small Intestine

The presence of alcohol prevents the cells and membranes of the small intestine from absorbing food into the blood-

16 / THE IMPACT OF ALCOHOLISM

stream. This interference causes the alcohol abuser to become deficient in vitamins, minerals, proteins, carbohydrates, and fats, all of which the body requires for health and well-being. These deficiencies may speed up the pathological changes within the brain and other organs.

Pancreas

An elevation of pancreatic enzymes indicates inflammation of the pancreas, another serious affliction which affects the alcohol abuser. After several years of excessive drinking, the painful condition known as pancreatitis may result.

When alcohol destroys the cells of the pancreas, they release potent enzymes. The enzymes escape from their normal ducts within the organ, destroying other pancreatic cells and causing them, in turn, to release their own enzymes. This chain reaction may result in massive destruction of the pancreas, a life-threatening condition which manifests itself by severe abdominal pain and shock.

A deficiency of pancreatic enzymes and a lack of insulin are symptoms of another form of pancreatitis from which alcoholics suffer. The tragic results of this condition are severe malnutrition or complications of diabetes.

Liver

Even small doses of alcohol cause pathological changes in the liver. This vital organ has the difficult task of metabolizing about 90 percent of the alcohol that an individual consumes. The liver then releases the remainder into the bloodstream. Thanks to the remarkable power of the body to restore itself, changes in the liver reverse themselves unless the individual continues to consume alcohol for a prolonged period of time. After several years of excessive drinking, the organ may undergo substantial and perhaps irreparable damage, including alcoholic hepatitis, the symptoms of which are inflammation of the liver and jaundice.

If the liver continues to suffer from acute inflammation

caused by alcohol, the final, deadly stage of deterioration, cirrhosis, may result. The organ makes a last, desperate attempt to repair itself by forming scar tissue. When alcohol kills liver cells, there are serious, irreversible consequences, such as the destruction of veins.

Heart

The heart, the very source of life, undergoes devastating damage from even moderate doses of alcohol. These changes are of the same nature as those of the liver. There is serious destruction of the tissue of the heart muscle. This tissue is replaced by useless fat, thereby decreasing gravely the effectiveness of this vital organ.

Alcohol kills the cells of capillaries, causing blood pressure to rise. Higher doses of the drug may result in myocarditis, a generalized inflammation of the heart. If the drinker continues to consume alcohol excessively, the heart may try vainly to repair itself by producing scar tissue, causing its life-sustaining performance to suffer severely. The organ may enlarge, and heart failure may be the consequence.

Genitourinary System

Alcohol may cause grave damage to the genitourinary system. Nephritis, an inflammation of the kidneys, results in the loss of critical body protein, including albumin and globulin, and red and white blood cells. A similar condition, cystitis, afflicts the urinary bladder. Both nephritis and cystitis will disappear if alcohol abuse ceases.

Sexual dysfunction may result from excessive use of alcohol, causing both physical and emotional distress. Excessive alcohol consumption causes enlargement and inflammation of the prostate glands, which leads to chemical prostatitis, a condition which decreases male potency.

When the drinker abuses alcohol chronically, there may be actual atrophy of testicular tissue. Sterility and a decrease in testosterone are the distressing results. When the male suffers

18 / THE IMPACT OF ALCOHOLISM

from a reduction of testosterone, he may develop feminine characteristics such as loss of pubic hair and, in some cases, the development of fatty breast tissue.

Many female alcoholics experience irregular menstrual periods, but usually, this situation reverses itself when alcohol abuse ceases. Far more serious are the consequences to the unborn. Excessive drinking gravely imperils the intricate development of the fertilized egg, embryo, and fetus. Spontaneous abortions, stillborn babies, and the deaths of infants within the first few days of their new and precious lives are very real risks for alcoholic mothers. Excessive drinking may also cause the tragedy of fetal alcohol syndrome, an irreversible condition in which there are gross abnormalities in the bones and muscles of the children. Their bodies are stunted and fail to develop beyond the age of about seven years. This needless calamity is the direct result of excessive alcohol consumption. Women who have borne children who are the victims of this syndrome may quit drinking and give birth to perfectly healthy infants.

Other Effects on the Body

Bone tissue suffers greatly from the injurious effects of alcohol. Heavy drinkers are frequently deficient in body proteins and calcium, resulting in brittle bones which fracture easily.

Bone marrow, the vital source of the creation of blood, is extremely sensitive to alcohol. Low white and red blood cell counts afflict alcoholics frequently, along with an abnormally small number of platelets as well. Because platelets are critical to the formation of normal blood clots, alcoholics may tend to bleed excessively.

Even the skin experiences detrimental effects from alcohol. A vast number of dermatologic conditions, including severe acne, loss of body hair, and a variety of rashes, trouble the heavy drinker.

Relatively small amounts of alcohol can impair the reflex

function of the diaphragm and voice box. This is a particularly dangerous effect of the drug, because it can cause the drinker to aspirate vomitus, resulting in chemical inflammation of the lungs.

Although many people ascribe numerous positive effects to alcohol, the drug actually does absolutely nothing beneficial for the human body. Rather, it is extremely destructive and causes significant pathological changes when it is abused over a period of time. This discussion has included only part of the detrimental effects of alcohol. There are many others, the details of which are beyond the scope of this chapter.

Intoxicated States

There is a great deal of individual variation in sensitivity and tolerance to alcohol. Overall responses, however, usually follow a definite pattern in most people. Even small doses of ethyl alcohol can adversely affect the central nervous system, resulting in the impairment of vision and other basic functions. Anyone who consumes too much of the drug will become intoxicated, whether he is an alcoholic or a social drinker.

The laws of most states consider a person to be intoxicated when he reaches a blood alcohol level of 0.1. At this point, a drinker may slur his speech and have difficulty in coordinating his movements. The forebrain controls these operations, and it suffers impairment when this much alcohol is present in the body.

When the drinker reaches a blood alcohol level of 0.2, the forebrain undergoes a more severe loss of its ability to function normally. The motor cortex suffers also, and the drinker may be quite unable to control his movements.

At 0.3 blood alcohol level, most persons become stuporous. Although the pulse, respiration, and blood pressure remain fairly normal, there is grave danger that the drinker may vomit and inhale the vomitus into his lungs, resulting in a chemical pneumonia which could be fatal.

If an individual reaches a blood alcohol level of 0.4, he enters the life-threatening state of alcoholic coma. The brain stem monitors and controls vital life functions, and at this point it becomes depressed and causes a hazardous decrease in the respiratory rate, a fall in blood pressure, and a concomitant rise in pulse rate. When a person enters this state, a true emergency exists. Strict medical monitoring is necessary, for respiratory failure and circulatory collapse may otherwise result in an end to life.

Unless a drinker has built up an extreme tolerance for the drug, death will almost certainly be the consequence of reaching a blood alcohol level of 0.5.

Pathological intoxication and alcoholic paranoia are two extremely serious conditions which require examination. Victims of pathological intoxication are usually young males who have suffered a head wound. The condition is often the result of a brain injury. It may also be a convulsive disorder. These persons may become violent and/or homicidal after only two or three drinks. Such behavior is a great danger to them and to society.

Alcoholic paranoia causes a person to become extremely suspicious of others and to lash out at them with undeserved tirades and accusations. An alcoholic may experience this condition months after taking his last drink. Treatment often includes the administration of psychotropic drugs, psychological support, and even hospitalization.

Withdrawal Syndromes

When a drinker becomes physically and psychologically dependent on alcohol, withdrawing from it may be a painful and even dangerous experience. The central nervous system has grown used to the depressant effect of the drug, and when alcohol use ceases, the brain, spinal cord, and nerves suffer from hyperexcitability.

The following syndromes all indicate that a drinker is the victim of alcohol addiction. Although they are separated for the sake of convenience, considerable overlap and a mixture of symptoms exist during the withdrawal process.

Psychomotor Agitation

This syndrome, more commonly referred to as "the shakes," usually affects the alcoholic anywhere from four hours to one or two days after he takes his last drink. When the depressant effects of alcohol are no longer acting upon the central nervous system, an abnormal stimulation results, producing muscular and glandular discharges which manifest themselves by hand tremors and shakiness. Electrical impulses pour furiously from the central nervous system, causing a highly excited state in all organs, tissues, and glands of the body.

As a result, the drinker usually suffers from general irritability and gastrointestinal distress. The pulse increases and blood pressure and respiratory rate rise. Stimulation from the adrenal and thyroid glands causes further symptoms, and an abnormal number of electrical discharges to the optic fibers may produce visual sensations and distortions.

The motor cortex of the brain becomes hypersensitive, producing an excessive number of nervous tissue responses which cause muscular contractions and cramping.

Abnormal psychological symptoms also plague the alcoholic. He may suffer from an unexplainable terror of answering the door or the telephone, and will often complain of a generalized anxiety in which vague, unspecified fears distress him.

This syndrome may so disable the alcoholic that it becomes necessary to help relieve his symptoms through the use of "minor" tranquilizers, or drugs which allow his central nervous system to withdraw more gradually from the depressed state to which it has become accustomed.

Alcoholic Convulsions

These frightening and perilous convulsions are of a grand

mal type, and usually affect the alcoholic one or two days after he takes his last drink. After seventy-two hours, he can consider himself safe from these life-threatening episodes. Dangerous complications such as swallowing the tongue may arise during a convulsion, making it imperative that competent medical personnel render treatment during these seizures.

Alcoholic Hallucinosis

These hallucinations are usually auditory and often take the form of maligning or threatening voices. The drinker may, for example, have the eerie experience of hearing someone call his name when he knows he is alone. He may hear doorbells ringing when no one is there, music when the radio is off, or telephones buzz when there is no one at the other end of the line.

Tactile hallucinations may also affect the alcoholic. He suffers from the sensations of ants or spiders crawling over his skin or cobwebs on his face. He tries vainly to brush them away. His hands, feet, and tongue may seem too large for his body, even though he can see plainly that they are normal.

The frightening symptoms of this syndrome usually appear between one and two days after the last drink.

Delirium Tremens

This is the most dramatic and serious of the withdrawal syndromes, and usually occurs three or four days after the last drink. Terrifying visual, auditory, and tactile hallucinations torment the victim, along with a variety of other symptoms, including severe fever, profuse perspiration, and rapid heartbeat. Infections may affect the body during this period, causing complications or even loss of life.

The victim loses all touch with reality. He believes that his horrifying world of hallucinations actually exists, and his memory becomes vague and confused.

An alcoholic who is undergoing the dangerous syndrome of delirium tremens must receive treatment in a hospital setting from competent medical personnel. Without such attention, between 10 and 15 percent of the victims will die.

Antabuse

Is there a weapon that can help the alcoholic in his battle with his illness? What can doctors do to ease the path to freedom from addiction?

Antabuse is one drug that offers help during the arduous recovery process. After a drinker takes Antabuse, any alcohol that he consumes will react violently with the substance, causing pain and discomfort. Doctors may prescribe it as an adjunct to treatment, although it definitely is in no way a substitute for treatment itself. The Federal Food and Drug Administration classifies Antabuse as a drug, but many experts in the field of alcoholism prefer to think of it as an "antidrug."

Antabuse reactions vary greatly from one person to another, both in intensity and the sequence of symptoms. Some individuals have only a mild response when they drink alcohol while Antabuse is in their systems. Others are so sensitive to the drug that they experience unpleasant reactions as long as several months after their last dose. They may even suffer from dull headaches or nausea when they come in contact with such innocent preparations as aftershave lotions, deodorants, or mouthwashes, all of which contain alcohol.

Most people, however, fall within a normal range in their reactions to Antabuse. A dosage as small as seven cc's (about one teaspoonful) of ethyl alcohol can cause a significant response to Antabuse.

Flushed, red skin is usually the first symptom of a reaction. A throbbing headache follows, becoming progressively worse as the reaction continues. The patient may be short of breath or experience an unpleasant constriction in his chest. He may even suffer severe chest pains which are frighteningly similar to the symptoms of a heart attack.

Nausea and vomiting, severe abdominal cramping, diarrhea, and other unpleasant gastrointestinal symptoms cause great distress for the patient. Generalized muscle cramping may also be present. The blood pressure rises slightly at first, but as the reaction continues, it declines again. A drinker should seek medical help at the first sign of an Antabuse reaction.

Antabuse does cause side effects which may trouble some users. There may be an allergic response, and in rare cases, a patient may develop a psychotic reaction which causes him to become paranoid and to suffer from auditory hallucinations. Less serious are complaints of a metallic taste in the mouth and a metallic body odor.

Antabuse is not for every alcoholic. Because the drug causes the blood pressure to rise and fall, a person with heart disease should not receive it. Individuals with esophageal varices run the risk of vomiting and causing a rupture, and victims of severe cirrhosis are also poor candidates for Antabuse therapy.

Antabuse, like other drugs, may react adversely with certain substances.

Antihistamines and vitamins C and A, for example, may counteract the drug and prevent a reaction. The physician should warn his patient to avoid any substance which might prove dangerous.

Antabuse therapy offers psychological support for the alcoholic as he works to become comfortable in his recovery program. The drug provides valuable insurance against impulsive drinking while tissues heal and the body returns to normal.

Stress and anxiety within the family may dissolve in the comfort of simply knowing that the alcoholic is relying on Antabuse. A calm, relaxed atmosphere at home helps speed the recovery process.

The ravages that alcohol inflicts upon the body do not disappear quickly. Antabuse therapy usually lasts about a year, for it takes at least this long for the body to repair the physiological damage and return to normal. Some experts in the field now believe that treatment with Antabuse should last two years, allowing the individual time to heal psychological wounds as well.

The physician may request a three-month contract with his patient, with the drinker agreeing to use the drug faithfully during that time. After ten or eleven weeks, patient and physician decide together whether to continue Antabuse therapy.

During the first three months of treatment, it is helpful if a loved one administers the daily dose of Antabuse to the alcoholic. This creates a psychological contract between the two in which the alcoholic promises his loved one and himself that he will not drink for that day. At the end of three months, the patient should become independent enough to take his own Antabuse, making a psychological contract in which he promises no one but himself that he will not drink.

It may be helpful if the daily dose of Antabuse becomes part of his regular routine. Most recovering alcoholics receive prescriptions for vitamins, and taking the Antabuse at the same time he swallows the vitamins will encourage a daily behavior pattern.

Antabuse is clearly not the answer to sobriety. It does, however, offer psychological support during the early, difficult phase of recovery.

CHAPTER **III**

Personal and Emotional Aspects of Alcoholism

Steven F. Bucky, Ph.D.

People drink alcohol because it makes them feel good. Two or three ounces of whiskey take away pain, guilt, and fear of personal inadequacy. The drinker feels that he is sitting on top of the world. If he continues to consume alcohol until he becomes intoxicated, he experiences a sense of warmth, expansiveness, and well-being.

This fleeting and deceptive euphoria results from the depressant action of alcohol on the central nervous system. A few drinks produce a blood alcohol level of 0.05 percent in an average-size person. Even this low concentration of the drug decreases the functions of the upper-most levels of the brain, seriously diminishing judgment, inhibitions, and restraint.

The loss of normal inhibitions prompts the drinker to act impulsively. He takes reckless personal and social liberties of which he might otherwise heartily disapprove, or he may talk ceaselessly and feel that he is quite witty and appealing.

As the concentration of alcohol increases, the lower motor area of the brain becomes dulled. Next the entire motor area begins to suffer, leading ultimately to the point where the drinker neither knows nor cares what is going on around him. If he insists on consuming even more alcohol, he may lapse into a coma. His lower brain centers may lose their ability to control breathing and other vital functions, and his very life may be threatened.

Alcohol has a wide and unpredictable range of effects on different individuals. It may cause a person to say and do things that he would never consider under normal circumstances. He might become totally uninhibited sexually or grow unexpectedly hostile and aggressive. Many variables contribute to the responses of different individuals to alcohol, including the strength of personal inhibitions and social conditions which influence behavior.

Common Personality Characteristics

Alcoholics differ from each other as greatly as do any other complex human beings. There is no "alcoholic personality." People who suffer from the crippling effects of alcohol abuse do, however, frequently exhibit a number of common characteristics:

1. *Overdependency*
   Many alcoholics never received the love and attention which are the birthrights of every child. This lack of warmth and affection stunts the delicate growth of emotional development, and they cling desperately to a parent or spouse, looking in vain to the other person for satisfaction, rewards, and positive feelings.

2. *Inability to Express Emotions Effectively*
   Alcoholics are often highly sensitive individuals who stifle their true feelings, especially their anger and hostility. These turbulent emotions simmer beneath the surface till they finally burst forth in unpredictable explosions.

3. *Emotional Immaturity and Low Frustration Tolerance*
   Alcoholics are often excessively moody, with feelings that range unaccountably from deep melancholy to extreme happiness.

PERSONAL AND EMOTIONAL ASPECTS / 29

4. *Ambivalence toward Authority*
   Problem drinkers may resent exceedingly having someone tell them what to do or being in a position where they must follow orders. Yet at the same time, they hunger for someone to take care of them.

5. *Grandiosity*
   When alcoholics drink, they feel like supermen or -women. They believe they are invincible, particularly in the delicate areas of interpersonal and sexual relationships. When they act according to this false sense of infallibility, they become extremely vulnerable to emotional wounds and misery.

6. *Perfectionism and Compulsiveness*
   Problem drinkers may insist imperiously that their way of doing things is superior to all others. They become childishly upset when other people refuse to do exactly what they wish in precisely the manner in which they want it done.

7. *Low Self-Esteem and Depression*
   Problem drinkers experience distressing feelings of worthlessness. They are certain that no one understands or cares about them, and believe secretly that perhaps they do not deserve anything better.

8. *Feelings of Isolation and the Inability to Form Close Interpersonal Relationships*
   Alcoholics find it difficult to establish and maintain the kind of deep, lasting relationships which offer security and refuge from the turmoil of life. The frightening voids in their existences cause them to feel painfully isolated and alone.

9. *Sex Role Confusion*
   Many alcoholics suffer agonizing uncertainty about their masculinity or femininity. Their desperate attempts to establish a firm sexual identity may lead them into activities which society deems inappropriate or undersirable, such as promiscuity, homosexuality, impotence, or frigidity.

It is important to remember that although these characteristics are common to many alcoholics, they do not occur in all problem drinkers. There is no typical alcoholic personality, and it is dangerous and inaccurate to ascribe a general set of behavior patterns to a particular individual.

Other Emotional and Behavioral Issues

Many people seek refuge and comfort during periods of extreme anxiety and conflict in the tranquilizing effects of alcohol. At first, the drug offers a sense of relief from tension. When the drinker begins to rely more and more heavily on alcohol, however, he may be trapped in an insidious, vicious circle of anxiety: he drinks to quiet his emotional conflicts and suffers painfully from guilt caused by his excessive consumption. He then seeks relief from his distress by drinking even more.

As alcoholism progresses, the drinker has increasing difficulty tolerating any kind of anxiety and tension. By the time he reaches the middle phase of the disease, he may be unable to face even the normal stresses of day-to-day living without the numbing effects of alcohol. In the later stages, the entire personality of the drinker may be swallowed in a murky abyss of alcohol. The drug controls the thoughts and actions of its victim, engulfing completely even the characteristics which originally led to excessive drinking.

The Reactive Alcoholic

A reactive alcoholic is one who becomes preoccupied with drinking only after suffering some overwhelming personal crisis. The dejected individual who seeks escape in the bottom of the bottle is a familiar and tragic picture. Trouble begins when the person finds the relief for which he was searching and then continues to rely on alcohol to shield him from pain and fear. In other cases, the drug merely intensifies depression, plummeting the drinker farther into the depths of misery. Unaware that alcohol has become the source of his woe, the individual drinks with even more desperation.

As the drinker continues to consume increasingly greater amounts of alcohol, he develops a physiological dependence on it. Trapped in a vicious cycle, he must continue to drink heavily to avoid withdrawal symptoms.

Some reactive alcoholics drink to blur their perceptions of an emotionally threatening environment. They find their lives so unpleasant and dissatisfying that they cannot function without the crutch of alcohol.

Perhaps the most common reactive alcoholic is the individual who drinks to break down psychological barriers which otherwise imprison him. He may be so uncertain that others like and accept him that he cannot have a good time at a party until he has taken a few drinks. Other people are unsure of their professional abilities and feel they must drink to perform successfully in their jobs.

Reactive alcoholics usually are productive and reasonably adjusted individuals before they fall prey to heavy drinking. They fulfill responsibly their obligations to their families, jobs, society, and to themselves. They achieve their educational objectives and often have rewarding and stable jobs. Until alcohol begins to interfere, their lives usually progress steadily toward reasonable goals.

Drinking begins to destroy happiness and productivity when the individual can no longer handle the stress life brings and turns to alcohol for relief. In some cases, the alcoholic may become so preoccupied with drinking that all other parts of his life lose their importance.

Alcohol and Emotional Disorders

When an alcoholic quits drinking, family and friends may blithely expect all problems to vanish along with the last hangover symptoms. They rejoice in anticipation of a new life

32 / THE IMPACT OF ALCOHOLISM

free from trouble and distress.

Usually this is a vain hope. Among other problems, there are cases where a severe, long-standing personality disorder surfaces when the individual quits using alcohol. Other people may experience a complex interplay of psychological and physiological factors which make emotional adjustment extremely difficult. The following are a few of the serious problems which may become visible as the clouds of alcohol dissipate into sobriety. Some are the direct result of excessive alcohol consumption, and others may have been part of the personality of the individual before drinking began.

Wernicke's Syndrome

This severe psychosis is the tragic result of the degeneration of nervous tissue in the brain. The individual is usually suffering from extreme vitamin B deficiency. The syndrome develops slowly, and symptoms include temporary visual problems, difficulty in controlling voluntary muscles, sleep disturbances, and hallucinations. Happily, only a small percentage of alcoholics are the victims of this disabling problem.

Korsakoff's Syndrome

Both mental and physical symptoms plague the victim of this syndrome. Perhaps the most serious sign of the disorder is confabulation. The individual unconsciously creates a story to fill in frightening major gaps in his memory. This unusual form of amnesia seems to bear a relationship to polyneuritis (inflammation of the nerves). The person suffers from terrifying disorientation and cannot remember who he is, where he is, or how he got there.

Antisocial Personality

The person with this disorder cannot form or maintain meaningful interpersonal relationships. He manipulates those close to him and can interact with them only in a superficial,

PERSONAL AND EMOTIONAL ASPECTS / 33

shallow manner. The individual who suffers from this personality defect is extremely preoccupied with himself and may get into trouble with the law because he behaves in unacceptable ways. Such people are often called "psychopaths" or "sociopaths."

Passive-Aggressive Personality

Individuals who suffer from this disorder are reluctant or unable to express their feelings directly. They become extremely passive outwardly, relieving their hidden hostilities through indirect rebellion, which may take the form of procrastination or doing the opposite of what their supervisors or families are expecting.

Passive-Depressive Personality

These individuals suffer from feelings of helplessness, isolation, and loneliness. Trying desperately to alleviate their misery, they manipulate those around them into constantly taking care of their selfish wants and needs.

CHAPTER **IV**

Legal Aspects of Alcoholism

*Douglas Harry, LL.B., and
Steven F. Bucky, Ph.D.*

Drinking and driving are a lethal combination. The drunk driver imperils not only himself, but all those with whom he shares the highway as well. In his hands, an automobile becomes a deadly weapon, and anyone he encounters may be his innocent victim. His reckless behavior is often responsible for immeasurable suffering and misery.

Every state has laws designed to discourage citizens from mixing alcohol with driving. Penalties for violating these laws are usually severe, for society recognizes the serious threat that the drunk driver poses. The purposes of criminal laws are to:

1. Punish the offender
2. Rehabilitate the offender
3. Deter crime

Laws governing alcohol abuse do not always accomplish these goals, but they do provide some means of controlling the drunk driver. This chapter deals with these laws, the need for them, and the procedures that officials use to enforce them.

Tests Measuring Alcohol in the Body

There is a great need for good laws governing the use of alcohol, and perhaps more importantly, for effective methods of enforcing them. The tests described here help police determine if a person has been drinking so much that it is dangerous for him to drive. The law requires that any person who uses the highway must submit to these tests if officials decide there is doubt about his sobriety.

The Breathalyzer

This test measures the alcohol content of the lungs, using a device known as a "gaschromatograph." An illuminated board (Cathode Ray Scoreboard) presents the results immediately. Most people (95 percent) take the breath test because it is quick and convenient.

The Blood Test

Officials take a sample of blood and measure the percentage of alcohol that is present in it.

Urinalysis

The percentage of alcohol in the urine can also reveal whether a person has been drinking too much to drive safely. The law requires that the individual void his bladder and then provide a second sample for analysis.

Driving Offenses Related to Alcohol

Driving while drinking is always dangerous. Sometimes, however, the consequences are more serious than at other times, and the law recognizes different offenses for which the drinking driver may be responsible. The following paragraphs apply specifically to California.

Misdemeanor Drunk Driving

A person who is guilty of this offense is driving "under the influence," but has not yet injured anyone else. "Under the influence" means that an individual has had enough to drink so that he has lost the sharpness of mind necessary to drive safely, as well as enough muscular coordination to lessen reaction time. If the blood alcohol level of the suspect is .10 or above, the law considers him to be definitely "under the influence." A level of .05 through .09 may, however, be high enough to charge him with DWI (Driving While Intoxicated) if he walks unsteadily, his eyes are dilated, or he exhibits other telling clues that he has had too much to drink.

The courts can convict a person of misdemeanor drunk driving even if he is not "legally drunk." If he has consumed enough alcohol to impair normal driving ability, the law considers him to be a menace, and he is guilty of the charge. This offense carries a maximum penalty of six months in prison plus a $500 fine (in California).

The U.S. Constitution requires that officials have "probable cause" before seizing a person. Therefore, an individual who is driving in a safe, lawful manner runs little or no risk of being stopped for drunk driving. If a person is driving erratically, however, doing such things as weaving in and out of traffic or using his brake light excessively, he gives officers reason to suspect that he has been drinking heavily.

After police stop an offender, they must determine whether or not to charge him with driving "under the influence." One way to do this is to ask him to submit to a field sobriety test which measures physical coordination. The driver walks heel to toe, touches his forefinger to his nose with eyes closed, or performs some other task requring normal physical dexterity. Such a test is voluntary and the law does not require the offender to tak part in it because many flaws exist in such an examination. Normal physical coordination for one person may be quite different for another and may depend on many factors besides consumption of alcohol.

If the police do charge the suspect with driving "under the influence," they advise him of his rights according to the rules set forth in *Miranda vs. Arizona* and then take him away to jail or to facilities for further testing.

According to the law, simply driving on a public street gives implicit consent to a chemical test for blood alcohol level. Technology has advanced to a point where these tests, properly administered, are quite accurate and revealing. If an officer arrests a driver and he refuses to submit to the test, the Department of Motor Vehicles may automatically revoke his license for six months without benefit of judicial process. Besides the inconvenience of losing his license, the offender must still face the original charge of driving "under the influence."

Laws governing drinking and driving are tough ones. They help with the vital task of guarding the safety of the public, and breaking them leads inevitably to a great deal of trouble.

It takes a surprisingly small amount of alcohol to raise the level in the bloodstream to the danger point. Approximately seven one-ounce drinks may produce legal drunkenness in a 160 pound man. If a bartender or host measures one-and-one-half ounces of liquor into the drinker's glass, only four drinks will plunge him into a state of legal drunkenness.

A person who makes a habit of consuming more than ten drinks on a single occasion may easily have a serious alcohol problem. The reverse of this statement is not true, however, and a person may be suffering from a hidden problem with alcohol even if he limits himself to less than ten drinks.

There is some evidence to suggest that more than 50 percent of the drivers who are responsible for the 50,000 fatal accidents each year have been drinking. A significant percentage of them were roaming the highways in the dangerous state of legal drunkenness (blood alcohol level = .1 percent or higher).

Felony Drunk Driving

If a driver injures someone while he is drunk, he becomes guilty of a felony. Even if he is so intoxicated he no longer knows what he is doing, the law considers him to be capable of having the intent to commit the crime.

Penalties for this very serious offense vary from state to state, but often the driver receives a prison sentence as well as having to pay a large fine. His automobile insurance rates skyrocket as well (see Table 2, page 40).

Implied Consent and Plea Bargaining

The courts must ultimately decide whether or not a defendant is guilty or innocent of a drunk driving charge. If he enters a guilty plea, or if the court convicts him, he faces severe penalties for his offense. Because of the seriousness of the charge, the law states clearly that a guilty plea must be a knowing, intelligent waiver of the right to a trial, and the defendant must understand fully the consequences which will result from his guilt.

There is such a multitude of misdemeanor drunk driving cases that a jury trial for each one would utterly clog the judicial system. Therefore, the district attorney or city attorney may plea bargain with the defense counsel, speeding up greatly the cumbersome legal process. The attorneys confer on the case, weigh the evidence, review the police report and chemical tests, and then try to determine between themselves the guilt or innocence of the defendant. This process gives both the state and the accused an opportunity to yield to the demands of the other if doing so would be in the best interests of everyone concerned.

In some cases, a prosecuting attorney will accept a guilty plea to a lesser offense even if he has a strong case against the defendant. Perhaps the evidence against a driver is convincingly substantial, including a high blood alcohol level and several credible witnesses who saw him fall out of his car. Yet he has an excellent driving record with no previous convictions, and he agrees readily to attend an alcohol education program or a remedial driving school. In such a case, an expensive court process would probably be far less effective than these methods of education and rehabilitation.

Senate Bill 330 requires any California driver who is guilty of two alcohol-related offenses to undergo a full year of treatment. If the individual refuses to do so, he will lose his license to drive and may receive a sentence of up to one year in prison. The passage of this bill suggests strongly that legislators are beginning to see the wisdom of doing more than simply punishing drivers who are guilty of alcohol-related offenses.

The High Cost of DWI

Mere statistics cannot possibly reveal the misery and suffering that may be the heartbreaking price of drinking and driving. The following example, however, illustrates vividly the high monetary cost of a DWI conviction:

A twenty-four-year-old unmarried male drives a three-year-old Chevrolet Nova to work and home again. The distance he covers each day is about twenty miles. He has a good insurance policy which includes medical payments and liability, comprehensive, collision, and uninsured motorist coverage. Table 2 shows clearly that his annual rates will rise significantly if the court finds him guilty of driving while intoxicated. These increases will continue to burden him for three years.

TABLE 2

	Premium with DWI Record	Premium without DWI Record	Cost of DWI
City			
Houston	$ 653	$532	$121
Los Angeles	$ 991	$593	$398
Cleveland	$ 698	$419	$279
Charleston, W. Va.	$ 633	$377	$256
Raleigh, N. C.	$1032	$385	$647

Laws Governing Alcohol Abuse

The laws in the state of California which forbid a person to combine drinking with driving are very similar to those in other parts of the country. Here are some examples of these laws which illustrate the seriousness with which society views this irresponsible and dangerous behavior:

Section 23101—Felony Drunk Driving

It is unlawful for any person who is under the influence of intoxicating liquor and any drug, to drive a vehicle and disobey any law which causes bodily injury or death to any person other than himself.

Section 23102—Misdemeanor Drunk Driving

It is unlawful for any person who is under the influence of intoxicating liquor, or under the combined influence of intoxicating liquor and any drug, to drive a vehicle upon the highway.

Section 13352—Revocation of Driver's License

The Department of Motor Vehicles shall immediately revoke the privilege of any person to operate a motor vehicle upon receipt of a duly certified abstract of the record of any court showing that the person has been convicted of driving a motor vehicle while under the influence of intoxicating liquor.

Section 13353—Implied Consent

A. Any person who drives a motor vehicle upon a highway shall be deemed to have given his consent to a chemical test of his blood, breath or urine for the purpose of determining the alcoholic content of his blood if lawfully arrested for any offense allegedly committed while the person was driving a motor vehicle under the influence of intoxicating liquor.

B. The person arrested shall have his choice of whether the

test shall be of his blood, breath or urine, and he shall be advised by the officer that he has such a choice.

C. If such a person refuses, or fails to complete the test, the Department shall suspend his privilege to operate a motor vehicle for six months.

Laws Governing Possession of Alcohol and Drinking in an Automobile

Section 23121

No person shall drink any alcoholic beverage in any motor vehicle when such vehicle is upon any highway.

Section 23122

No person shall have in his possession, while in a motor vehicle, any receptacle containing an alcoholic beverage which has been opened.

Section 23123

It is unlawful to keep in any motor vehicle, upon any highway, any receptacle containing any alcoholic beverage which has been opened, unless such container is kept in the trunk or in some other area not normally occupied.

Section 23123.5

No passenger in any motor vehicle who is under the age of 21 shall knowingly possess or have under his control any alcoholic beverage.

Section 23126—Blood Test

If there was 0.10 percent or more by weight of alcohol in the person's blood, it shall be presumed that the person was under the influence of intoxicating liquor.

Section 40300.5—Arrest of Intoxicated
Driver without a Warrant

Notwithstanding any other provision of law, a peace

officer may, without a warrant, arrest a person involved in a traffic accident when the officer has reasonable cause to believe that such person has been driving while under the influence of intoxicating liquor or under the combined influence of intoxicating liquor and any drug.

Section 12805—Issuance and Renewal of Driver's License

The Department of Motor Vehicles shall not issue or renew a driver's license to any person who, because of excessive and continuous use of alcoholic liquors, is incapable of safely operating a motor vehicle, or who is addicted to the use of or is an habitual user of any drug to a degree that the person is rendered incapable of safely operating a motor vehicle.

Other Alcohol-Related Crimes and Accidents

A drinker does not necessarily have to get behind the wheel of an automobile to become involved in unnecessary accidents and violent crimes. An alarmingly high percentage of the problems of American society involve excessive drinking. Alcohol abuse plays a part in approximately 21 to 30 percent of deaths involving narcotics, suicides, and fatal aircraft accidents other than commercial or military. About one-third of sexually aggressive acts against women and nearly one-half of fatal auto injuries, drownings, and fights in the home involve alcohol abuse. More than 50 percent of all shootings, stabbings, homicides, deaths caused by fire, sexually aggressive acts against children, beatings, accidental poisonings, and arrests also involve alcohol abuse.[1]

The serious problem of alcohol abuse has grave consequences for all of society. Finding a solution will require the work and concern of everyone, not only those who suffer from a problem themselves.

CHAPTER V

Interpersonal Effects of Alcohol Abuse

Rosalie Jesse, Ph.D., Adrienne McFadd, Ph.D., Gloria Gray, Ph.D., and Steven F. Bucky, Ph.D.

Alcoholism is a family illness. Its destructive effects cause havoc in the lives of everyone who loves and cares for its victims. The disease may even haunt a family from generation to generation. Children from alcoholic families have a much greater chance of developing the illness than do youngsters with parents who are free of alcoholism.

Although the illness causes extreme disruption and distress to the activities and relationships which sustain family life, most people who suffer from the devastating effects of alcoholism delay far too long before seeking help. Family members will usually wait an average of nine painful, bewildering years before taking constructive action to deal with their problem. Without help, families often develop behavior patterns which actually encourage the progress of the illness. Each person becomes increasingly lonely, isolated, and frightened.

Family Life Suffers

Children need a great deal of love and attention from their parents to develop healthy personalities. A mother or father who is alcoholic, however, is far more concerned with his or her own selfish needs than with those of the child. He or she becomes preoccupied with receiving love rather than giving it. The alcoholic parent may be dependent, helpless, and afraid, making it impossible for the child to rely on him or her or look to the parent for guidance. Yet the alcoholic mask of arrogance, hostility, and resentment completely disguises these feelings of inadequacy. The alcoholic makes unreasonable demands on everyone, both economically and emotionally, and without help, family members have no weapons with which to defend themselves.

Life becomes totally unpredictable. Discipline is inconsistent, and the family shares fewer and fewer good times together. The disease creates an unstructured family crisis, causing continual uneasiness and fear. The guidelines and patterns for feeling and behavior which are necessary for stable personality development vanish in a quagmire of alcohol.

Family members usually respond to this crisis with precisely the wrong reactions. They make a desperate attempt to deny the problem and then, realizing the utter futility of such an effort, they try to hide the drinking for as long as possible. At last, admitting defeat, they struggle to seek help, and are often unsuccessful in their quest.

The Alcoholic Father

A family in which the father is alcoholic makes a number of unsuccessful attempts to adjust to its painful problem. At first, his sporadic bouts of heavy drinking acutely embarrass both him and his wife, but each tries hard to minimize the problem. As his drinking becomes more frequent, his wife suffers deep shame and humiliation. She makes a vain effort to protect her loved ones by isolating them from social contacts and situations which may involve drinking. She feels intensely guilty and inadequate as a marriage partner, believing that the problem must be her fault. She tries unsuccess-

INTERPERSONAL EFFECTS OF ALCOHOL ABUSE / 47

fully to stop her husband from drinking by hiding his liquor and monitoring his expenses and declares that if he really loved her, he would stop abusing alcohol.

By now, however, her husband has completely lost control of his drinking. Life becomes chaotic. The children suffer agonizing guilt and fear over the violent arguing and fighting that goes on between their parents, and they become the innocent victims of the social stigma which society places on alcoholism.

As the father grows increasingly dependent on alcohol, his work performance suffers, and the family may undergo severe financial hardships which force the wife to go to work outside the home. The alcoholic may desert his family for prolonged periods in a desperate effort to escape during his drinking episodes.

Life grows rapidly more and more unstable, causing both parents to suffer extreme emotional conflicts. The alcoholic, trapped hopelessly in the insidious net of his drinking, finds his situation bewildering and cannot understand why his life has become unmanageable. He becomes terrified that he is going insane and contemplates suicide. Unless he receives treatment, he is helpless against his overwhelming compulsion to drink. Yet he may refuse the life-saving aid he requires. The situation may grow so impossible that it becomes necessary to remove the children from the home, with or without the non-alcoholic parent.

When separation or divorce looms ahead, the impending crisis often motivates the alcoholic to seek help at last. His decision will not, however, cause all the problems in the family to vanish miraculously. If he receives inpatient or residential treatment, the family will once again be left alone. When sobriety comes through the help of Alcoholics Anonymous, the nightly meetings will severely limit the time he has to spend with his loved ones. During this turbulent period, it is important that the spouse and children seek the support of Al-Anon and Alateen. Few programs exist, however, for children below the age of twelve, and parents must make a special effort to take time to offer the help these young children need.

When the alcoholic becomes sober at last, new and unexpected difficulties suddenly materialize. Parental roles begin to shift back to what they were before heavy drinking began, causing adjustment problems for both father and mother, and bewilderment and confusion for the children. Before his initial recovery, the children may have regarded their father with varying degrees of pity, affection, and disillusionment. Mother had adopted the authoritarian role, and they had begun to see her as "head of the house." Now they must readjust themselves to view their parents in more traditional roles.

To his wife, the alcoholic seemed like a recalcitrant child. She communicated her attitudes of fear and contempt for her spouse to her children and may have deeply resented the affection the youngsters displayed for their father during his intermittent periods of sobriety.

During the time when alcoholism ravaged the family, the children felt a desperate need for the love and attention of their mother. She, however, was preoccupied with her alcoholic spouse and failed to give them the warmth and affection they craved, making them feel painfully rejected. At other times, the mother may have lavished affection on the bewildered youngsters, causing them to become innocent targets of the jealous rage of their father.

The oldest son may have shouldered many of the responsibilities of his father, and the alcoholic, sensing the vital loss of his masculine role, may have lashed out with sadistic brutality at the boy, derogating him and punishing him unjustly. Because they lack a stable, admirable male role model, these boys tend to identify with the safety and security of their mothers. Yet fear of the disapproval of their fathers causes them to deny vehemently, to themselves and others, that these feelings exist. This ambivalence toward sexual identity often haunts these children throughout their lives.

Daughters also experience deeply ambivalent feelings toward their alcoholic fathers. Their emotions range from hate to love to fear, causing them bewilderment and confusion. Even though daughters may side with their mothers, earnestly declaring their loyalty, they may be troubled by the vague, disturbing feeling that their mothers are somehow to blame for the drinking problem.

While a daughter often escapes from the hostility vented by her father, she may be the innocent victim of his incestuous seduction. This shattering, devastating experience may create an unnatural bond between them in which they align together against the mother. The daughter suffers excruciating remorse because another part of her still loves and depends upon her female parent. She may be troubled further by the erroneous belief that she is the only one who can influence her father, which causes her to feel even more guilt and remorse when he continues to drink.

The Alcoholic Mother

The reported incidence of alcoholism among women is creeping steadily upward, but it is still considerably less than among men. This may be because there are many women who manage successfully to hide their drinking from the world, at least temporarily. Free from the restrictions of a job outside the home, they spend long, lonely days drinking alcohol and remain undiscovered by society. These unhappy women usually begin drinking with the utmost secrecy, buying their bottles with money saved from the family budget. For quite some time, a woman may be able to continue to manage her household duties while she engages in her furtive affair with the bottle. Her husband and friends may be quite unaware of her growing problem. Although the husband senses vaguely that something is wrong and the marriage is deteriorating, he will usually accept the explanation that his wife is simply overworked.

The alcoholic woman cannot hide her problem forever. When her heavy drinking becomes painfully apparent at last, her husband may righteously abandon her. The wife of an alcoholic usually will move heaven and earth to help her husband, but the reverse is not true. A husband is often disgusted and repulsed by the alcoholic behavior of his wife, and his love for her dissolves in a fog of anger and recriminations.

If the husband begins to view his wife with such loathing that he deserts her, the children may become overly dependent upon their mother. Fearing desperately that they will lose her as well, they cling more and more tightly to her and develop a fierce sense of protection toward her. They tend to lie to others about their home life, fabricating pleasant images of a mythical family which bears no resemblance to their own. Gradually they begin to withdraw from the world of school and friends, becoming more and more isolated and miserable.

The helplessness their mother exhibits forces older children to shoulder the heavy responsibility of caring for younger brothers and sisters. When the father does remain dutifully at home and assumes the care of his children, the mother often displays jealousy and rage. She becomes childishly spiteful and competes for the attention of her husband. In some cases, an older daughter may begin to assume some aspects of the "wife role" in her relationship with her father. This further enrages the mother, who feels a deep threat to her femininity.

The behavior of the mother becomes unpredictable, ranging from violent hostility and aggression to morose sentimentality. Following a drinking bender, she may suffer extreme remorse, and in an effort to compensate for her behavior, she becomes maudlin and overindulgent with her children. At other times, she is impatient and punitive. She is extravagant and deceitful, putting her own selfish needs ahead of those of her family. The children suffer deeply from the constant tension of never knowing what to expect from her.

When the mother is drinking, she jeopardizes continually her own safety and that of her children. She may fall and injure herself, drop lighted cigarettes, or clumsily break dishes and furniture. The children become so fearful for her that they maintain a constant, lonely vigil to protect her, refusing to leave her even to go to school or out to play. During the periods when the mother is not drinking, she suffers from severe hangovers. She feels sick and depressed and demands continual sympathy.

If there is an infant in the family, the mother begins to neglect him dangerously. Totally wrapped up in her own selfish concerns, she forgets to feed him, leaves him wet and cold, or slaps or beats him if he continues to cry. Older children suffer from such devastating humiliation and insecurity that they refuse to bring playmates home. Bewildered and confused, they believe their mother is a worthless drunk and that because they come from such a blighted family, they themselves will never amount to anything.

Effects of Alcohol Abuse on the Spouse

The relationship which suffers most harshly from the ravages of alcoholism is the marital one. The spouse becomes as hopelessly enmeshed in the insidious web of the disease as the alcoholic himself. Because of this deep involvement in the problem, some experts call the spouse a "co-alcoholic." The disease wreaks destruction upon all that is dear to the spouse, including family life, sexual relationships, economic resources, the well-being of the children, and status within the community. Marriage partners share a common world, and when this world darkens and grows stormy for one spouse, the other suffers as well.

Marriage with an Alcoholic Spouse

During the painful years when alcoholism is developing, the

spouse learns to adapt her behavior to the unreasonable demands of the alcoholic. Sometimes the partners establish this destructive pattern even before marriage, resulting in an acceleration of the process. Her responses to him become so automatic that when he enters treatment, the entire marital relationship undergoes radical disruption. In cases where the drinker continues to refuse help, the marriage usually ends painfully in separation, divorce, psychiatric hospitalization, or the tragic death of the alcoholic.

No marriage is quite like any other, including unions in which one partner is alcoholic. There are, however, patterns which seem to appear frequently in these relationships.

Experts have painted various pictures of such marriages. A common one includes an alcoholic husband who is passive and dependent and relates to his wife in an immature, hostile manner. His dependency may satisfy her own need to be dominant, causing her to encourage his drinking in order to make herself seem strong by comparison and to justify her deep feelings of anger and resentment.

Some professionals describe the partners in a marriage of this kind as a hyperfeminine male and a dominant, aggressive, masculine female. Others suggest that some wives of alcoholics have a masochistic need for punishment or suffer from severe self-doubt and a desire to rescue the alcoholic partner.

Theories such as these imply that the dependency of a husband and his alcoholic deterioration satisfy certain selfish needs within the personality of the wife. Some clinicians have described women who cannot adjust to the sobriety of their husbands, or who seduce them with bottles of whiskey. Personality dynamics of this kind would help to explain the massive denial, rationalization, and projection that often exist among the wives of alcoholics, as well as their common resistance to treatment.

Many wives of alcoholics, however, have healthy personalities before the onset of the drinking problem. They find themselves searching desperately for effective ways to respond to increasingly stressful conditions. Some wives even develop psychosomatic symptoms as a result of their efforts to cope with a situation against which they are powerless.

When the wife is the alcoholic, special difficulties appear. Her housewife role gives her ample opportunity to drink in secret, so her problem may progress dangerously before anyone discovers it. Husbands may choose to look the other way as the drinking increases, withdrawing into their jobs to create distance between themselves and the alcohol problem. These men may become overprotective and treat their wives as if they were children, or ignore them sexually.

When the woman alcoholic's illness progresses to the point where she can no longer hide it, she suffers far more acutely from the social stigma of her problem than does her male counterpart. Society disapproves much more heartily of heavy drinking in women than in men. To further complicate the problem, her husband often resists taking part in her treatment.

There is some indication that a high proportion of alcoholic women have interests which society categorizes as "masculine," while their husbands display interests which society views as "feminine." This clash with expected role behavior may cause further conflict.

Universal Effects of Alcoholism on the Spouse

Each person chooses his own way of coping with the problems which besiege him. Many spouses of alcoholics, however, suffer from common difficulties, and often they seem to develop similar behavior patterns and ways of responding to the frightening situation in which they find themselves.

Alcoholism weaves a complicated web of conflicts which ensnares the spouse as well as the drinker. Sometimes a spouse joins the alcoholic and drinks with him. Other wives may covertly support the problem to satisfy inner needs of their own. Some respond aggressively, insisting that they can handle things while they attempt to force the alcoholic to stop drinking.

When all solutions fail, a spouse may quietly acquiesce to the illness or escape from it by ending the marriage. Both these alternatives are born of desperation and helplessness. Equally destructive are behavior patterns of denial, withdrawal, or plunging into hopeless despair. The rapidly shifting and unpredictable behavior of the alcoholic may cause the spouse to engage in several fragmentary responses at once, with none of them providing any positive help.

Emotional Effects on the Spouse

The spouse of the alcoholic suffers acutely from deep shame and humiliation and a growing sense of personal inadequacy. She tries desperately to hide the problem, but she is often secretly convinced that the drinking is her fault. The wife of an alcoholic seems to feel this guilt and shame far more keenly than her husband does. Society has taught her that she is responsible for the happiness and well-being of her family. As the drinking increases, she suffers more and more from a crushing sense of failure.

As she tries desperately to cover up the alcohol problem, she cuts herself off from social contacts and activities, becoming more and more isolated. Her self-inflicted loneliness deprives her of the emotional support she needs, limiting her to the meager supply which still survives within the family.

Wives of alcoholics may suffer physical abuse from their husbands, or they may watch helplessly as their children are beaten or injured. Constant tension and fear result from this unsavory situation, but the wife may have no idea where to turn for help, or she may be too ashamed to do so. She develops a vast amount of inner hostility for which she cannot find an effective outlet. When the alcoholic is drinking, he ignores or rebuffs her, and when he is sober, he insists that her accusations are unjustified. This frustrating state of affairs may plunge the spouse into severe depression.

Sexual Effects on the Spouse and Marriage

In at least 55 percent of alcoholic marriages, both partners withdraw from the sexual relationship. The alcoholic may seek to prove his or her threatened masculinity or femininity by seeking out other sexual partners. The non-alcoholic spouse uses sex as a weapon, withholding favors as a punishment or trying to bribe the drinker into sobriety.

A passive, dependent, and sexually undemanding male alcoholic implicitly encourages his wife to be protective, nurturant, and sexually unresponsive. Female alcoholics may become promiscuous, believing they are unworthy of love and have nothing to offer but their bodies.

Husbands of alcoholics suffer from deep feelings of personal rejection. They may become hostile, lashing out against their helplessness to control the situation. Others adopt the same protective, sexually undemanding behavior pattern that many wives of alcoholics develop.

Social and Economic Consequences

Alcoholics are often unable to experience any satisfying interpersonal contact unless they are drinking. Their circle of friends dwindles to the dubious companionship of their drinking buddies. Non-alcoholic partners do not care to try to keep up with their drinking spouses, so they quit accompanying them to social functions.

The social life of the family may be further diminished by the increasing amount of money that the alcoholic squanders on liquor. The situation may even deteriorate to the point where there are no longer enough funds for basic necessities such as food and shelter. One member of an alcoholic family recalls waiting silently with his mother and brother for his father to come home from work on payday. They were usually disappointed, for the father often failed to appear till several days later when he ran out of money to buy another bottle. He would be on the verge of withdrawal, and the family would have to borrow rent money and subsist on potato chips. Eventually, some alcoholics lose their ability to hold jobs, contributing added hardships to the family.

The Marital Scenario: Probable Course of Events

Many alcoholic marriages follow a basic sequence of events. At first, the spouse and family do all they can to deny the problem, even to the point of idealizing the drinker. Or the spouse may recognize that a problem exists and try everything in her power to control the drinking. She may baby the alcoholic, rescue him from the consequences of his behavior, or punish and recriminate him. The spouse may pressure the alcoholic to drink moderately, hide liquor, or keep careful track of any money he spends. Often she combines all these responses in a desperate effort to curtail the drinking, even while she continues to deny the problem to the outside world. She becomes the victim of severe inner stress from trying to manage this paradoxical coping effort.

During the middle stages of the illness, there is severe emotional and social disorganization. The spouse and family isolate themselves because of limited funds and shame. The sexual relationship suffers disruption, and the spouse may withhold sex in a hopeless attempt to combat the drinking behavior. All the important roles that the alcoholic played are taken over by the spouse, and she finds herself the only dominant adult left in the family structure. During the later part of the middle stages, the sense of helplessness that the spouse experiences may become so acute that she seeks outside assistance from a parent, clergyman, or counselor.

Finally, there will be some culminating event or crisis which triggers an emotional turn of events for the spouse. She experiences a profound sense of futility and feels that the situation is hopeless. Realizing at last that the problem will not go away, she begins to act more decisively. She may seek divorce or separation, or force the alcoholic to hospitalize himself. Some wives even resort to entering a hospital themselves, using the "patient" role to avoid dissolving the marriage.

Once the spouse becomes convinced that she can do nothing to change the situation, she begins to exclude the alcoholic from the activities and affection of the family. This may cause the male alcoholic to react violently. He may even attack his wife and children physically. Most wives experience fear of physical abuse quite late in the alcoholic process. Some have lived for years after their divorces in fear of their husbands returning to assault them.

Some spouses may deteriorate into alcoholics themselves. This is one way that a marriage partner can continue to preserve the disintegrating relationship, at least temporarily.

The final reorganization of the family, then, may or may not include the alcoholic, and in a few instances, the spouse may no longer be part of the family either, resulting in total disintegration. The most positive possibility is that the alcoholic will undergo treatment, be reintegrated into the family, and resume an effective partnership with the spouse.

During the alcoholic experience, the spouse tries various methods of coping with the mounting life crisis. One of the most frightening aspects of the whole experience is the unhappy realization that not only is the alcoholic a different person from the fantasized one which the spouse believed him to be, but also that she herself is far less capable of dealing with the problems of life than she assumed. A therapy team, after working intensively with couples with alcoholism, suggested that a spouse (male or female) who is living with an alcoholic generally feels a degree of inadequacy or failure. He or she turns away from the alcoholic and looks for emotional support elsewhere. It is often difficult for these persons to learn to understand that alcoholism did not cause all their problems.[1]

Effects of Parental Alcohol Abuse on Children

Family Structure

Because alcoholism causes distress and misery for all family members, it is important that they are not neglected in the frantic attempt to help the drinker. Children of alcoholics suffer from numerous emotional and behavioral disorders, and they run a grave risk of becoming victims of the disease themselves. About 50 percent of all alcoholics come from families in which the illness affected at least one parent.

Treatment almost always centers around the alcoholic, the spouse, and perhaps the teen-age offspring, while younger children are usually forgotten. There is a real need to intervene in the lives of these sadly neglected youngsters while there is still time to break the vicious alcoholic cycle of which they may so easily become victims.

It is important to understand how devastatingly disruptive the problems of alcoholism are to normal family processes. It was stated earlier that most families wait an average of nine years to seek help after a parent first begins to show signs of trouble with alcohol. This long, painful period affords plenty of time for the family to create destructive patterns of interaction which eventually become self-perpetuating.

General Characteristics of Children in the Alcoholic Family

Although children of alcoholics do not suffer universally from precisely the same problems, there are certain general patterns which affect a large number of them. Many of these children act in an unstable, unpredictable manner. This may lead to deleterious social behavior which results in problems with the police and courts, difficulties at school, and poor interpersonal relationships. An abnormal amount of dissension among siblings, hostility, fear, and lack of trust usually exist in these families. The youngsters suffer deeply from destructive feelings of guilt, inferiority, and alienation, but they usually externalize their emotional conflicts. They are also the victims of more serious illnesses and accidents than children from non-alcoholic families.

As the youngsters go through various stages of development, different clusters of problems appear. They suffer from serious illnesses and accidents during infancy and early childhood. This may be because the alcoholic parent dangerously neglects his or her children, leaving them extremely susceptible to such problems. Other difficulties also trouble them during this vulnerable period. These include sleep disturbances and difficulties with eating and eliminative functions. The children may vent their hostility by throwing temper tantrums, or they may become hyperactive.

Throughout middle childhood, or from the ages of about seven through twelve, a normal youngster begins the important social process of forming and consolidating friendships. The early adolescent is a member of two distinct worlds: the world of adults and that of his peers. Each of these worlds offers him crucial experiences in his daily life which help to mold his subsequent development. The child of an alcoholic, however, usually suffers from such deep embarrassment over his circumstances that he feels alienated from his peers. Thus, he loses a vital element in the process of his development. Insecurity, fear, and lack of trust may severely limit his relationships. He reacts by withdrawing into himself or by turning outward his helpless frustration and hostility, which results in aggressive, antisocial behavior. Both alternatives are equally destructive, intensifying his already low self-esteem and confirming his feeling of inner worthlessness.

Sometimes a child may try desperately to defend the alcoholic parent or tell lies to the outside world in a pitiful attempt to create an image of his family which bears no relationship to reality. He worries excessively and becomes preoccupied with what he perceives to be his insurmountable problems. His work at school suffers, causing additional frustration. A first experience with alcohol abuse often occurs during this period of extreme emotional strain.

When the child reaches the turbulent period of adolescence, he begins to use alcohol more frequently. He may also become involved with using other drugs abusively.

Defiance and hostility are normal occurrences during the storms of adolescence, but in the children of alcoholics, such emotions are much more intense than in other youngsters. These teen-agers usually direct their anger and frustration toward parents and other authority figures, resulting in antisocial behavior and problems with the law. Because these youngsters allow their school work to slip during the preteen years, they cannot make up their losses, and they continue to be poor students. Thus, school loses its meaning and importance for them. Undue sexual anxiety and role confusion plague these adolescents, often resulting in promiscuity.

These problems affect male children somewhat differently than females. More boys than girls are the victims of accidents or illnesses. Boys tend to become aggressive, rebellious, and extrovertive, while girls withdraw into shyness and self-negation.

Why do a frightening one-half of the children of alcoholics later become victims of the illness themselves? What is it in these youngsters, who certainly have become painfully aware of the hazards of alcohol abuse, which leads to their own uncontrolled drinking? Many experts have pondered this question, and no one has discovered a conclusive answer. Approaches to the problem include psychological (personality), genetic (inherited), and sociological (cultural) theories.

The biosocial theory is an eclectic view which includes aspects of all three approaches. Adherents of this theory believe that persons may inherit a physiological predisposition toward the illness. This tendency greatly increases their chances of developing the disease when they are exposed to the right set of environmental factors, especially the frustration of having to cope with an alcoholic environment as a child.

Children who later become alcoholics often exhibit certain behavior patterns and personality conflicts at a very young age. Thus, early identification may be possible, greatly increasing the chances of interrupting the alcoholic cycle within the family. The recovery and abstinence of the parent do not solve the myriad of problems alcoholism brings with it. The entire family must receive help to change their thinking and behavior.

Female Alcoholics: A Comparison to Men

During the past few years, the number of women who are referred for treatment for alcoholism has been increasing steadily. The latest statistics suggest that there are more than a million women in the United States who are victims of the disease. Until recently, most researchers in the field of alcoholism dealt with the male drinker. With the dramatic increase in women who need treatment, more and more studies are exploring the special problems of being alcoholic and female. Some of the results of this new research suggest some interesting patterns.

Women alcoholics, like their male counterparts, often come from families in which at least one parent, usually the father, suffered from the disease. These women may see their mothers as cold and domineering and their fathers as weak and passive. This distressing view of their parents often causes later conflicts with their own femininity. They may also suffer from excessive anxiety and poor self-concepts, and, as a result, they fail to develop effective social skills.

Usually, women become problem drinkers at a later age

than do men. They experience more emotional instability and find it much easier to hide their problem from society and their families.

A more detailed description of these special problems follows:

Drinking Patterns

Several differences exist in male-female drinking patterns. Women are usually secret drinkers, hiding their problem behind the closed doors of their homes. They present a socially respectable outward appearance and rarely get into trouble with the law or come to the attention of officials. Husbands, family members, friends, and even physicians overlook or deny their excessive drinking, believing this kind of problem happens only to others.

Women prefer distilled spirits or wine rather than beer. They are usually older than men when they begin drinking heavily, but once alcoholism develops, it progresses more rapidly.

Figure 2 (page 63) suggests that men in higher socioeconomic groups do slightly more drinking than those at lower socioeconomic levels. The drinking rate for women is much higher in the upper socioeconomic groups. Heavy drinking patterns, however, bear absolutely no relationship to socioeconomic level.

Figure 3 (page 64) indicates that males suffer from a significantly higher number of alcohol-related problems than women do. These data may be misleading, however, because women manage to hide their problem much more effectively.

FIGURE 2

PERCENT OF DRINKERS AND HEAVY DRINKERS
AMONG ADULTS, BY AGE, SEX, AND SOCIOECONOMIC LEVEL
U.S.A. 1964-1965

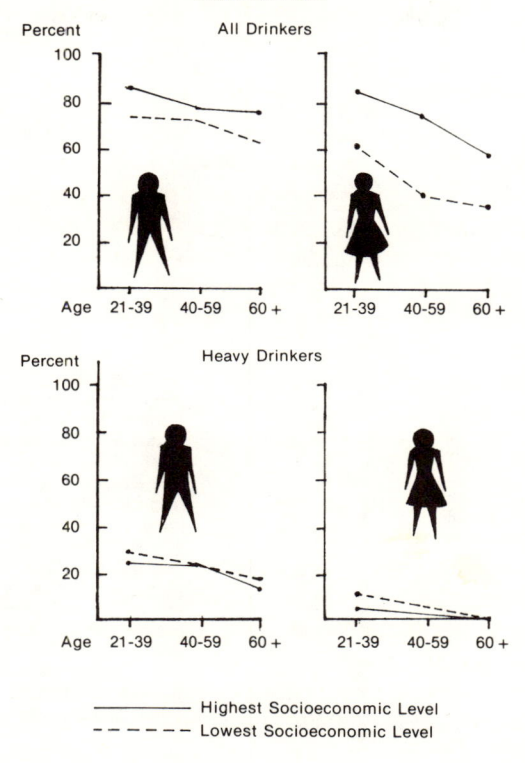

——— Highest Socioeconomic Level
- - - - - Lowest Socioeconomic Level

NOTE: Reprinted from *First Special Report to the U.S. Congress on Alcohol and Health,* Publication 74-68 (Rockville, MD: Department of Health, Education, and Welfare, 1971).

64 / THE IMPACT OF ALCOHOLISM

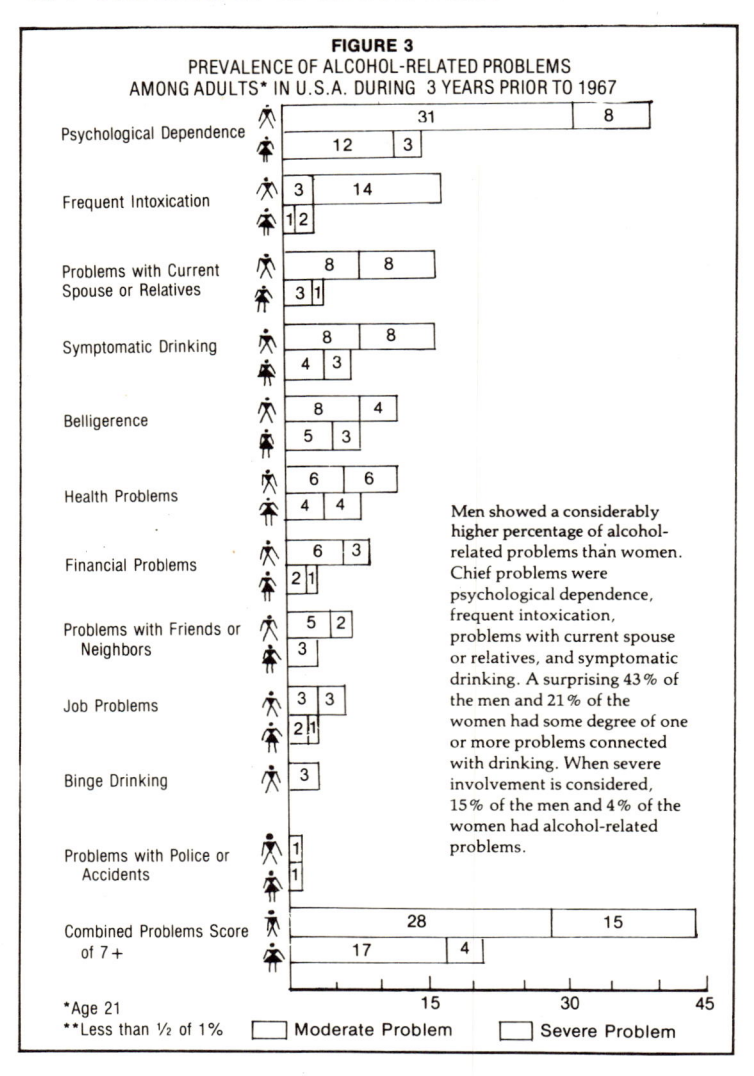

FIGURE 3
PREVALENCE OF ALCOHOL-RELATED PROBLEMS
AMONG ADULTS* IN U.S.A. DURING 3 YEARS PRIOR TO 1967

Problem	Men	Women
Psychological Dependence	31 / 8	12 / 3
Frequent Intoxication	3 / 14	1 / 2
Problems with Current Spouse or Relatives	8 / 8	3 / 1
Symptomatic Drinking	8 / 8	4 / 3
Belligerence	8 / 4	5 / 3
Health Problems	6 / 6	4 / 4
Financial Problems	6 / 3	2 / 1
Problems with Friends or Neighbors	5 / 2	3
Job Problems	3 / 3	2 / 1
Binge Drinking	3	
Problems with Police or Accidents	1	1
Combined Problems Score of 7+	28 / 15	17 / 4

Men showed a considerably higher percentage of alcohol-related problems than women. Chief problems were psychological dependence, frequent intoxication, problems with current spouse or relatives, and symptomatic drinking. A surprising 43% of the men and 21% of the women had some degree of one or more problems connected with drinking. When severe involvement is considered, 15% of the men and 4% of the women had alcohol-related problems.

*Age 21
**Less than ½ of 1%   ☐ Moderate Problem   ☐ Severe Problem

NOTE: Reprinted from *First Special Report to the U.S. Congress on Alcohol and Health*, Publication 74-68 (Rockville, MD: Department of Health, Education, and Welfare, 1971).

Hormonal Differences

The same dose of alcohol produces a higher blood alcohol level in women than it does in men. Women experience greater variability in blood alcohol level as well. This may be because men have a higher percentage of water in their bodies than women do, causing the alcohol to become more diluted.

The menstrual cycle, with its accompanying changes in sex hormones, affects the way the body handles alcohol. During the premenstrual period, when levels of estrogen and progesterone decline, a given dose of liquor will cause a higher blood alcohol level than at other times during the monthly cycle. Men appear to exhibit no such fluctuations.

Social Perspectives

More men than women struggle with academic problems and social difficulties before they become heavy drinkers. About 30 percent of male alcoholics had serious problems in school, while only 20 percent of women experienced such difficulties. Men get into trouble with the law because of alcohol abuse more frequently than women, and men have more auto accidents when they are drinking. More men than women lose their jobs (40 percent of men compared to 20 percent of women) because of alcohol abuse.

Socioeconomic levels seem to affect the kinds of problems that alcoholism causes for women. Lower status alcoholic women suffer from the same difficulties as men do, perhaps because many of them are working, while higher status women usually remain hidden and protected in their homes.

Both men and women alcoholics experience distressing and disruptive incidents during their childhoods. More women, however, seem to suffer from such episodes, especially before the age of sixteen, and females more often report destructive relationships with their parents. Their mothers are dominant, rigid, unforgiving, and perfectionistic. They offer no love and support to their bewildered daughters, but remain emotionally distant from them. Fathers, who may be alcoholic, are usually warmer and more responsive, but they are also weak and ineffectual, particularly in their relationships with their wives. It is not surprising that a daughter who struggles to grow up in a devastating environment like this often suffers from feelings of extreme worthlessness, insecurity, and inadequacy.

When such a woman marries, she chooses a husband who displays the same destructive personality characteristics as her mother. Thus, she perpetuates the distressing patterns of interaction which disrupted her childhood. The lack of warmth and affection during her early years creates a powerful need for love, but she is pathetically unable to accept it when someone offers it. Because she was never able to express her hostility toward her parents in a positive manner, she did not learn to deal effectively with other frustrations. The only way she knows how to escape from her problems is through alcohol.

Pathology

The woman alcoholic is the victim of crippling psychological problems, including severe depression, guilt, and anxiety which may lead to suicide attempts. She suffers from disturbing feelings of inadequacy, inferiority, and a pervading sadness, as well as low levels of self-esteem. Drinking fails to provide the solace she is seeking so desperately, and she remains confused, miserable, and unhappy even while intoxicated.

For men, the primary problem that accompanies alcoholism is sociopathy and antisocial behavior patterns. About 25 percent of males with a drinking problem have this personality defect. In these men, drinking usually begins at a younger age than in other alcoholics, and their first hospitalization occurs earlier. They suffer from more personality disorders and have more difficulties with their marriages. The prognosis for their recovery is poor.

Sex Role Identity

Many alcoholic women experience sex role conflicts. They suffer from a myriad of difficulties in the area of feminine identification and female role performance. The resulting conflicts contribute greatly to their drinking problems.

Sex role consists of those behaviors which the culture expects from a person simply because he or she is male or female. Although stereotypes are changing, society still encourages women to be nurturing, passive, and dependent and to find their personal satisfaction in a home and children. Men, on the other hand, should be assertive, independent, and competitive. They should seek rewards from a career outside the home and provide comfortable financial support for their families.

Sex role identity describes the personal sense of maleness or femaleness which an individual experiences. The expectations of society are responsible for many of the ideas a person develops about masculinity and femininity, and when an individual suffers conflict between what society expects and what he or she feels inside, confusion and trouble may result.

Studies by Wilsnak suggest that when women drink heavily, they lose their desires to be powerful and assertive.[2] Unlike a man, a woman does not drink to increase her sense of power, but to enhance her feelings of femininity and womanliness. Unfortunately, she soon discovers that the men in her life see her alcoholism as anything but attractive and feminine.

A relatively high incidence of obstetrical and gynecological disorders affect female alcoholics before the onset of excessive drinking. Many of these women experience a specific life crisis, often in the area of feminine role performance, shortly before alcohol abuse begins.

These findings suggest that sex role conflicts often trouble the female alcoholic. There may be a bewildering clash between the traditional feminine behavior which society expects of her and her own unconscious desires. Because society has shaped her conscious feelings about femininity, this conflict may cause her to suffer grave doubts about her womanliness. Crises such as obstetrical and gynecological problems, divorce, and other related difficulties may rapidly deepen her fears about herself. She begins to drink in a desperate effort to restore her feelings of feminine adequacy.

Changing Attitudes

The women's liberation movement has had great impact on the whole dilemma of sex role. Before the movement became widely accepted, fewer women aspired toward traditionally masculine achievements such as career success. Now, many women are questioning the old feminine role and the severe limitations it imposes on them. More and more women are engaging in careers and other traditionally "masculine" behavior. Blazing new paths, however, is never easy, and these women may feel a very real conflict between the desires brought about by their increased awareness and the "feminine" behavior they were brought up to believe made them womanly.

This new view of the role of women has brought with it still other complications. While society used to frown on a woman drinking at all, it has now become quite acceptable for women to use alcohol. One positive result is that women are much more free to admit they suffer from a drinking problem than they were in the past.

A series of studies conducted over the past ten years indicates that there has been an alarming rise in the use of alcohol among adolescents, especially teen-age girls. Because most drinking problems have their roots in adolescence, the increase in alcohol use and abuse among the young will probably result in higher rates of alcoholism among adults. Since the percentages of young women users have risen more drastically than those of young men, the next decade may produce a tragic increase in female alcoholism.

CHAPTER VI

Effects of Alcohol Abuse on Work Performance

Steven F. Bucky, Ph.D.

Alcoholism costs business and industry a tremendous amount in lost money, time, and efficiency. The Christopher D. Smithers Foundation describes the effects as a "four billion dollar hangover." There are about six and one-half million alcoholics in the United States,[1] and only 3 to 5 percent of them are on skid row. A significant percentage of the rest are on the payrolls of the nation, collecting regular checks despite the appalling costs to their employers.

The "four billion dollar hangover" figure includes losses from excessive absenteeism, tardiness, and sick leave, misuse of fringe benefits, wasted time and materials, accidents, inefficiency, bad judgments, generally poor work performance, and the investment made in training persons who are unable to continue in their jobs. Many other indirect costs result from alcohol abuse. Salesmen cannot relate effectively to customers, causing public relations to suffer. Supervisors waste valuable time in a hopeless attempt to curb the problem through disciplinary measures. The company must keep extra records, and moral weakens as other employees see the alcoholic getting away with inappropriate behavior.

Recent figures suggest that alcoholism may afflict as much as 8 to 10 percent of the work force. "According to a conservative estimate made by The National Council on Alcoholism, the only non-profit health agency working in the field, business and industry employ over 2,000,000 sufferers of alcoholism whose out-of-control drinking keeps them off the job a total of thirty-six million work days a year. In addition there are millions of abnormally heavy drinkers who drag through millions of unproductive hangover days as 'half-men' (a term originally applied to such employees by the Yale Center of Alcohol Studies)."[2]

The Alcoholic Worker

The alcoholic employee often presents a frustrating mixture of poor work one day and excellent performance the next. His personality ranges from extremely pleasant to abominably disagreeable. At times he works with dedicated zeal and dependability, and at other times he is negligent and ineffectual. The bewildered supervisor never knows what to expect. When he believes he has put up with all that he can, his problem worker appears to snap out of his difficulties and once again becomes an asset to the company.

The executive who is alcoholic causes severe and often irreparable problems for his organization. Lost in a haze of alcohol, he makes poor decisions which sometimes result in damage that lasts for years. He may appear on the surface to be functioning well, but the alcoholic fog which surrounds him prevents him from communicating effectively with others, resulting in a severe morale problem for all those who work with him.

On-the-Job Signs of Alcoholism

One of the earliest signs of alcoholism that affect work performance is the familiar hangover. When they become frequent and severe, a wise supervisor should suspect trouble. Symptoms include thirst, headache, fatigue, nausea, and jitters. Hands tremble, and on-the-job accidents become frequent. The worker usually tries to hide his suffering, however, taking care to stay away from his peers or supervisor.

Other symptoms which may be warning signs of encroaching alcoholism are upper respiratory difficulties, including pharyngitis and bronchitis, as well as gastrointestinal distress such as acute gastritis, colitis, diarrhea, and duodenal ulcers.

As the illness continues its insidious progress, the individual begins to drink surreptitiously, trying his best to prove to himself and others that nothing is wrong. He goes often to the bathroom and takes unusually frequent or lengthy "coffee" breaks. He develops a complicated network of excuses, explanations, rationalizations, and lies to justify his abuse of alcohol.

Distribution of Problem Drinkers

Problem drinkers cause difficulties in all phases of business and industry. Approximately 38 percent are skilled laborers, sales personnel, or are in service-related areas. About 33 percent are unskilled laborers and personnel, and 27 percent are owners, managers, and professionals.[3]

Observation of Symptoms by the Supervisor

A supervisor should be able to notice several telling symptoms in an employee who abuses alcohol. During the early stages of alcoholism, he continually slips away from his designated work place, offers unusual excuses for absences, or experiences regular mood changes after lunch. The quality of his work becomes poor and his eyes may be red and bleary. As the disease continues its crippling progress into the Crucial Stage, the alcoholic becomes erratic, working at an uneven pace, and the quality of what he produces deteriorates even further. He arrives at his job with frequent hangovers. When the illness reaches the Chronic Stage, the individual begins to take mysteriously long lunch breaks. He is drinking secretly over the noon hour, and afterward he tends to talk louder and may suffer from hand tremors.

The alcoholic sinks rapidly into a maelstrom created by alcohol. He begins drinking during working hours and avoids other people, hoping vainly that no one will notice his bizarre behavior. His face is often flushed, and he pretends to suffer from numerous minor illnesses in an effort to make excuses for his absences.

Realization of Symptoms by the Alcoholic

The alcoholic himself is aware that something beyond his control is taking over his life. He notices the same disabling symptoms in himself that his supervisor has observed, though at a different pace.

During the Prodromal Stage, he has an almost chronic hangover which causes him to be nervous and jittery. His hand trembles and he is continually miserable.

When he reaches the Crucial Stage, his eyes are red much of the time and his edginess and irritability increase. He withdraws into himself, avoiding both his peers and his supervisors.

In the Chronic Stage, the individual is hopelessly lost in the depths of his compulsion. He drinks constantly, beginning before he leaves home in the morning and continuing throughout the working day. He is often absent, and he is aware that his excuses are weak and unconvincing. He comes in late, slips away whenever he can during the day, and departs early in the evening. His lunch periods become suspiciously long and he begins to use breath purifiers, hoping desperately that no one will notice he smells of liquor. Extreme changes of mood trouble him, and he realizes that the quality and quantity of his work have suffered tremendously.

Even though he is frighteningly aware that the symptoms he is experiencing mean he is in trouble, he is helpless to fight against his abnormal drinking behavior. He sinks deeper and deeper into the quagmire of his illness.

Symptom Progression

In 1951, E. M. Jellinek outlined the progression of symptoms in the disease of alcoholism. His descriptions are still valuable today in understanding the illness.

During the early phase, the individual has an increased tolerance for alcohol. His ability to drink more than others pleases him greatly, for he believes it indicates he is physically superior to others. He uses alcohol frequently to relieve tension and anxiety, and he rapidly develops a sense of urgency about taking the first drink. During this period, he experiences his first frightening blackouts, or alcoholic amnesia. He feels deeply guilty and confused.

When he reaches the Crucial Stage, he drinks in the morning and makes the terrifying discovery that he is unable to stop. In a vain attempt to deny his guilt and fear, he becomes aggressive and grandiose. His use of alcohol begins to obsess him. Towards the end of this phase, he may exert a tremendous effort to stop drinking. He fails dismally. He procrastinates, finding it difficult to begin new tasks. Distressing physical symptoms begin to manifest themselves, bewildering and confusing both the alcoholic and those around him.

During the Chronic Stage, vague, indefinable fears begin to plague the individual. He is unable to keep his thoughts in order, making it difficult even to lie consistently about his alcohol use.

Towards the end of this phase, the individual comes to the terrifying realization that he is indeed an alcoholic, and he is powerless to change himself or his situation. Once he weathers this crisis, he begins to move toward treatment. For the first time, he honestly wants help, realizing that it is his only hope for survival. He has difficulty asking for help, however, and suffers from painful feelings of ambivalence about his decision to stop drinking. In an effort to reconcile his conflicting emotions, he may begin attending AA meetings or start to participate in individual or group therapy. His fears begin slowly to diminish and his self-esteem rises encouragingly.

He loses his antisocial need to withdraw from others and begins the difficult readjustment to his family, co-workers, and supervisors. He develops new interests, and as time goes on, he becomes comfortable and happy in his new-found sobriety. He reaches out to others, beginning at last to trust them and accept their limitations.[4]

Abstinence alone does not solve the complex web of problems created by alcoholism. The individual must find new and positive ways of dealing with all of his interpersonal relationships while he continues to work on his drinking problem. This is a slow, difficult process, requiring a great deal of effort. Problems do not disappear miraculously when the alcoholic gives up the bottle.

CHAPTER VII

Treatment

Steven F. Bucky, Ph.D., et. al.

It is vital that the alcoholic receive treatment if he is to arrest his illness and commence his recovery. Very few alcoholics can escape on their own from the vicious, progressive, and fatal nature of this disease. Various forms of treatment are available, and the counselor must motivate and guide his patient to employ the treatment modality that suits the needs of each individual.

Alcoholics Anonymous

Jere Bunn

"Alcoholics Anonymous is a fellowship of men and women who share their experience, strength, and hope with each other that they may solve their common problem and help others to recover from alcoholism. The only requirement for membership is a desire to stop drinking. There are no dues or fees for AA membership; we are self-supporting through our own contributions. AA is not allied with any sect, denomination, politics, organization, or institution; does not wish to engage in any controversy, neither endorses nor opposes any causes. The primary purpose is to stay sober and help other alcoholics to achieve sobriety."[1]

The Alcoholics Anonymous Preamble explains succinctly what AA is. It is not an organization in the commonly accepted sense of the word, with structure, charter, bylaws, officers, directors, executives, and so on. It is, rather, a loosely-knit group of men and women who have banded together, as the Preamble says, for the sole purpose of helping others to stay sober and to carry the message of how they did so to other alcoholics.

Since its inception in 1935 with its first two founding members, Bill Wilson, a New York stockbroker, and Dr. Robert Smith, an Akron surgeon, AA has become worldwide. Active in nearly every country in the world, the membership is now well over 1,000,000.

Most nonmembers gain their impression of "how it works" from the literature and "open" meetings. While the open meeting reflects the more visible aspect of AA to the nonalcoholic, this is really the tip of the iceberg. Group dynamics, wherein the real AA therapy takes place, occur in the "closed" meetings, which only alcoholics can attend. Most researchers use two categories to refer to the alcoholic, "sober" and "drinking," focusing their attention on the very static view that the "absence of alcohol" constitutes being "recovered." AA recognizes the downward, progressive nature of the disease, and consequently stresses the upward progression required for recovery.

The real movement for the alcoholic away from his compulsion takes place in these closed sessions, at which times the "life experiences" of recovery are tied into the Twelve Steps of AA. It should be noted that only the First Step involves alcohol. The rest of the Steps deal with living a "spiritually sound" life.

The Twelve Step Program

The Twelve Steps of Alcoholics Anonymous are as follows:

1. We admitted we were powerless over alcohol—that our lives had become unmanageable.

2. Came to believe that a Power greater than ourselves could restore us to sanity.

3. Made a decision to turn our will and our lives over to the care of God *as we understood him.*

4. Made a searching and fearless moral inventory of ourselves.

5. Admitted to God, to ourselves, and to another human being the exact nature of our wrongs.

6. Were entirely ready to have God remove all these defects of character.

7. Humbly asked Him to remove our shortcomings.

8. Made a list of all persons we had harmed, and became willing to make amends to them all.

9. Made direct amends to such people wherever possible, except when to do so would injure them or others.

10. Continued to take personal inventory and when we were wrong promptly admitted it.

11. Sought through prayer and meditation to improve our conscious contact with God *as we understood Him,* praying only for knowledge of His will for us and the power to carry that out.

12. Having had a spiritual awakening as the result of these steps, we tried to carry this message to alcoholics, and to practice these principles in all our affairs.[2]

Each person must work the Steps in his or her own way. The following brief explanations of the Steps are offered by the author to help anyone who wishes to begin the process.

Step One—This step is the cornerstone on which the remaining eleven steps are built. The alcoholic must accept responsibility for his inability to predict his behavior or his control over his drinking once he consumes alcohol. Alcoholism is often described by AA as an allergy, coupled with a compulsion and an overriding obsession so subtly powerful that no human strength can break it. As a result of this powerlessness and because of the denial syndrome, an alcoholic blames other places, persons, or things for the many troubles he faces. Consequently, life becomes unmanageable.

Step Two—Ego or self-centeredness is one of the principal underlying problems that most alcoholics must face and deal with before recovery can begin. Lives may be in total disarray, but because of "skid row" stereotyping, which leads some to feel they are not "that bad yet," many feel they can do it alone. AA stresses the difference between religion and AA spirituality. Here is where the positive aspects of a hopeful attitude or self-fulfilling prophecy come into action.

Step Three—Once an alcoholic accepts his disease and realizes a life governed by self-will is a disaster, he makes the decision to accept a higher order of values, beliefs, and ideas. Again the emphasis is on the spiritual; consequently, *"God as we understood Him"* is translated into many forms and perceptions. To specifically address many of the blocks an alcoholic may have to this step, the book *Alcoholics Anonymous* discusses at length the "religion" issue, including a chapter entitled: "We Agnostics."

Step Four—A quote from *Alcoholics Anonymous* is important in understanding this step: "Our liquor was but a symptom. So we had to get down to causes and conditions."[4] Once an alcoholic identifies his character flaws, he can deal with them in an honest, open, and nonthreatening manner. Once he clears away the wreckage of the past, he can begin the process of personal growth.

Step Five—The alcoholic can deal with his terrible sense of isolation by sharing his inventory with God as he understands Him and another person. In the book, *Twelve Steps and Twelve Traditions*, the message is, "This feeling of being at one with God and man, this emerging from isolation through open and honest sharing of our terrible burden of guilt, brings us to a resting place where we may prepare ourselves for the following steps toward a full and meaningful sobriety."[3]

Step Six—This step involves the process of removing all doubt or reservations about change. "Entirely ready" is the key. Instant and complete transformation is neither expected nor even desired. To be *willing* implies a complete openmindness which allows for new knowledge to be acquired in order for change to take place—again using a spiritual approach which removes the center of the universe from inside the alcoholic and places it with his Higher Power.

Step Seven—The seventh step, which many AA members call the "humility" step, is a continuation of the effort of the alcoholic to change his attitude, thus permitting him to move out from himself toward others and a spiritual way of life. A quotation from *Twelve Steps and Twelve Traditions* illustrates this: "As we approach the actual taking of Step Seven, it might be well if we AA's inquire once more just what our deeper objectives are. Each of us would like to live at peace with himself and his fellows. We would like to be assured that the grace of God can do for us what we cannot do for ourselves. We have seen that character defects based upon shortsighted or unworthy desires are the obstacles that block our path toward these objectives. We now clearly see that we have been making unreasonable demands upon ourselves, upon others, and upon God."[4]

Step Eight—Using objectivity and avoiding extreme judgments about himself or others, the alcoholic writes a list of those people he has harmed throughout the course of his life. This step involves a lifelong process, as do all the steps, because as the alcoholic gains a greater degree of honesty and insight, the list of people he has harmed grows longer. Those he blamed previously for his condition are often at the top of his list. Again, willingness becomes a factor as the alcoholic makes a decision to make amends to everyone.

Step Nine—Probably one of the most action-oriented steps of the program, the ninth step is simply based on the theory that "faith without works is dead." The alcoholic must concentrate on his wrongs and in no way mention the wrongs others have done. One of the most important aspects of this step is to avoid injuring others. To make oneself feel better at the expense of someone else is considered wrong in AA. "There may be some wrongs we can never fully right. We don't worry about them if we can honestly say to ourselves that we would right them if we could .... We should be sensible, tactful, considerate, and humble without being servile or scraping. As God's people, we stand on our feet; we don't crawl before anyone."[5] This step is a powerful effort in socialization. It decreases greatly the feeling of isolation from which the alcoholic suffers.

Step Ten—Considered one of the primary maintenance steps, the tenth step requires the alcoholic constantly to review his strengths and weaknesses, preferably on a daily basis. By continually checking attitudes through the behavior of the day, the alcoholic can check dysfunctional actions before they become a form of habit.

Step Eleven—The eleventh step is the "power step." The alcoholic begins to construct a definition of his Higher Power based on love and happiness and free of "hellfire and damnation" ideas that many alcoholics brought with them into AA. The alcoholic must learn to communicate with his Higher Power, not through a ritualized form, but through honest, frank, and open dialogue. As some AA members claim, "Often man sent words to the heavens, but his thoughts remained on earth." The foundation of meditation is listening to the basic instincts of man. Many AA members consider these instincts to be the messages of God. The instinctive nature of man is a powerful tool, but the alcoholic has blocked it out with false rationalizations. Blending his instincts with his intellect and spirit brings to the alcoholic a real sense of freedom and power.

Step Twelve—By daily practice of the steps of AA, the alcoholic awakens to a sense of the spirit based on the fellowship of man that employs a faith outside of oneself. By carrying the message, the alcoholic not only can help others, he can also strengthen his own program of growth. Each AA member is encouraged to work with the practicing alcoholic. As some AA members say, "The best person to help someone through his seventh day of sobriety is one who is in the eighth day." The most important aspect of this step is the practicing of AA principles every day with everyone.

"We are careful never to show intolerance or hatred of drinking as an institution . . . . A spirit of intolerance might repel alcoholics whose lives we could have saved, had it not been for such stupidity . . . .

"After all, our problems were of our own making. Bottles were only a symbol. Besides, we have stopped fighting anybody or anything. We have to!"[6]

The Twelve Steps, which are the basic principles of AA, are the "how to" for the survival of the alcoholic. But without the Twelve Traditions, AA would undoubtedly go the same way as another group dedicated to the problem of alcoholism, the Washingtonian Group. Because of its involvement with politics and religion, this very worthwhile movement was destroyed.

The Twelve Traditions of A.A.

One—Our common welfare should come first; personal recovery depends upon A.A. unity.

Two—For our group purpose there is but one ultimate authority—a loving God as He may express Himself in our group conscience. Our leaders are but trusted servants; they do not govern.

Three—The only requirement for A.A. membership is a desire to stop drinking.

Four—Each group should be autonomous except in matters affecting other groups or A.A. as a whole.

Five—Each group has but one primary purpose—to carry its message to the alcoholic who still suffers.

Six—An A.A. group ought never endorse, finance, or lend the A.A. name to any related facility or outside enterprise, lest problems of money, property and prestige divert us from our primary purpose.

Seven—Every A.A. group ought to be fully self-supporting, declining outside contributions.

Eight—Alcoholics Anonymous should remain forever nonprofessional, but our service centers may employ special workers.

Nine—A.A., as such, ought never be organized; but we may create service boards or committees directly responsible to those they serve.

Ten—Alcoholics Anonymous has no opinion on outside issues; hence the A.A. name ought never be drawn into public controversy.

Eleven—Our public relations policy is based on attraction rather than promotion; we need always maintain personal anonymity at the level of press, radio, and films.

Twelve—Anonymity is the spiritual foundation of our traditions, ever reminding us to place principles before personalities.[7]

Al-Anon and Alateen

Alcoholics Anonymous was in the forefront in declaring alcoholism as a family disease that seriously affects the family and friends of the alcoholic.

These people may, in fact, need more assistance and counseling than the alcoholic if they are to launch an effective recovery program. While the stress is often on the alcoholic and his disease, the co-alcoholic has his or her own denial symptoms and false rationalizations that seriously distort his or her sense of reality. Consequently, the co-alcoholic must undergo the same changes the alcoholic does, but in a way that is his or her own. One of the basic rules is that the co-alcoholic must separate his or her problems from those of the alcoholic. This separation does not necessarily involve the person. While Al-Anon and Alateen both use the same Twelve Steps and Twelve Traditions that AA uses, they have their own closed meetings and programs, coming together with the alcoholic in only the open meetings.

In Al-Anon, the stress is on self, not the alcoholic. By observing several rules of thumb, the Al-Anon member can learn to deal with his or her own problems.

1. Learn all the facts and put them to work in your own life. Don't start with the alcoholic.

2. Attend A.A. meetings, Al-Anon meetings, and if possible, go to a Mental Health Clinic, Alcoholism Information Center, or a competent counselor or minister who has had experience in this field. Go yourself; don't send the alcoholic.

3. Remember you are emotionally involved. Changing your attitude and approach to the problem can speed up recovery.

4. Encourage all beneficial activities of the alcoholic and cooperate in making them possible.

5. Learn that love cannot exist without compassion, discipline, and justice, and to accept love or give it without these qualities is to destroy it eventually. [8]

Alateen is sponsored by Al-Anon, and each group uses a member of Al-Anon for guidance. They have their own closed meetings, again using the Twelve Steps and Twelve Traditions to change their own lives.

Other Kinds of Help
Steven F. Bucky, Ph.D.

Several other kinds of help are available to the alcoholic. The individual needs of each person must determine the kind of treatment which is best for him.

Outpatient Facilities

Outpatient psychotherapy offers help to the alcoholic who is making the difficult attempt to stop drinking or has already achieved initial sobriety. Unless alcoholism counseling or AA membership accompanies this psychotherapy, however, it usually proves futile.

This kind of treatment is useful for helping the drinker and his family to understand emotional and behavioral difficulties. Persons who receive discharges from inpatient and drug treatment services may also benefit from this type of help.

Outpatient services provide medical and psychosocial treatment, including individual, family, and group therapy, as well as chemotherapy. Participants in outpatient programs are usually in good physical health and are receiving the support of employers, family, and friends.

Inpatient Services

When an alcoholic becomes an inpatient, he generally stays at least two to four weeks in a hospital, spending each day engaged in activities designed to encourage recovery. Inpatient services are primarily for those who have definite medical requirements, or those who need a structured period of time to break the deadly cycle of dependence on alcohol. The staff assesses each patient individually and designs a treatment plan to suit his needs. An individual program may include films about alcoholism and lectures on the physiological, psychological, legal, and family aspects of the disease. The counselors who provide primary treatment are usually recovering alcoholics themselves, but particular emotional and interpersonal needs of the patient may require additional professional support.

Good inpatient programs return the alcoholic to his home or community as rapidly as possible. Usually, exposure to Alcoholics Anonymous, individual and group psychotherapy, and various forms of counseling are part of the overall plan. Staff members encourage patients to participate in these continuing forms of treatment when they leave the hospital.

Day Care Programs

Day care offers help to those alcoholics who have achieved initial sobriety but still need a highly structured environment to help them avoid slipping back into the trap of compulsive drinking. Day care programs encourage the alcoholic to break through his crippling denial and confront his problem openly. He can then begin the restorative process of changing his attitudes and behavior, which process is his only hope of learning to function effectively without alcohol. He receives encouragement and support when he tries to secure or maintain a job or engages in social activities.

Like inpatient treatment, the program usually includes films and lectures on the psychological and physiological effects of alcoholism, and individual and group counseling are available.

This kind of treatment offers a highly structured program to help the alcoholic maintain his precious sobriety during the daytime hours. When he goes home at night, however, staff members encourage him to participate in AA meetings. Day care may serve as an intermediate step between hospitalization and a complete return to normal community activity, or it may offer an alternative to inpatient care. This type of program reduces the costs of treatment significantly, because a day care facility can treat many more patients than a hospital of equal size. Day care offers support, therapy, and education, and helps with the important task of integrating the patient back into his family and community.

Alcohol Safety Action Program

Drunk drivers are a menace to society. Usually, however, simply punishing them with a jail sentence or imposing a fine does little to change their behavior. An educational program is sometimes able to accomplish what severe penalties cannot.

TABLE 3
FACES: EDUCATIONAL MODULES

1. Alcohol Use: Its Effects on the Individual and Society
2. Signs and Symptoms of Alcohol Abuse and Alcoholism
3. Alcoholism as a Disease (Physical Effects of Alcohol Use)
4. Alcoholism as a Disease (Intoxicated States and Withdrawal)
5. Alcoholism as a Disease (Use of Antabuse)
6. Behavioral Aspects of Alcohol Abuse
7. Personality Characteristics Associated with Alcohol Abuse
8. Alcohol Abuse and Its Emotional Impact on the Individual
9. Effects of Alcohol Abuse on the Spouse
10. Effects of Alcohol Abuse on the Children
11. Effects of Alcohol Abuse on the Family
12. Women: Alcohol Use and Abuse
13. Adolescent Drinking
14. Drug Abuse
15. Effects of Alcohol Abuse on Work Performance
16. Alcohol Abuse and the Law
17. Changing Attitudes about Alcohol Abuse and Alcoholics
18. Treatment Available to the Alcohol Abuser and the Alcoholic
19. Treatment: Alcoholics Anonymous (AA)
20. Treatment: Alanon
21. Treatment: Stress Reduction Training
22. Treatment: Psychodrama
23. Role Clarification after Achieving Abstinence
24. Communication Skills with Friends and Family
25. Group Dynamics
26. Review and Summary

There are numerous Alcohol Safety Action Programs throughout the country. In San Diego, Family Alcoholism Counseling and Educational Services (FACES) educates and counsels drunk drivers through a twenty-six week experience consisting of two sessions per week. Groups of twelve to fourteen participants learn about the legal, medical, and emotional aspects of alcoholism, as well as the devastating effects of the disease on family, spouse, and employers. During the first session each week, the group receives and discusses academic materials (sessions are listed in Table 3, page 86). The second weekly session consists of group counseling. Participants discuss alternative life-styles and provide each other with the mutual support they need to modify goals and change their destructive drinking behavior. They learn to be more effective in their interpersonal relationships and to find other ways of dealing with their frustrations besides abusing alcohol.

The primary purpose of such a program is to reduce traffic-related deaths, injuries, and property damage, but other goals include increasing the percentage of problem drinkers who come to the attention of courts and licensing agencies and ensuring that the legal system creates the greatest possible impact on abusive drinking behavior.

Detoxification Centers

A detoxification center offers a place of relative safety for an alcoholic to withdraw physically and psychologically from the deadly grip of alcohol. Staff members diagnose and evaluate the drinker during a two- to five-day stay, and then refer him to the kind of treatment that will offer him the most help.

Recovery Home

In a recovery home, an alcoholic who has achieved initial sobriety lives with his peers in a supportive, structured environment. He receives food, shelter, and some personal services during a one- to two-month program in which he makes the difficult and temporarily frightening adjustment to life without alcohol. He learns self-reliance and new ways of thinking while he participates in work, recreational and social activities, and group counseling.

Several other forms of therapy are also useful in fighting the disabling and insidious disease of alcoholism. The following sections describe three of these treatment modalities. They include:

1. Biofeedback—An effective method of reducing tension and anxiety in alcohol abusers.
2. Psychodrama—A type of therapy which offers new hope to those who are unable to maintain effective interpersonal relationships.
3. Power Motivation Training—A way to help those who need to feel more in control of themselves and their environments in order to deal assertively (not aggressively) with other people.

Biofeedback

David Jacobs, Ph.D.

Why do people continue to drink long after it is clear that to do so is utterly destructive? Alcoholics pay the heavy price of broken families, lost jobs, and ruined health and must live with the painful knowledge that they contribute heavily to the misery of others. Yet they continue to drink excessively, and their numbers grow frighteningly year by year.

People drink for many different reasons. Some lonely individuals use alcohol in a desperate attempt to find friends. They may hate the taste of liquor and may not even like the way alcohol makes them feel. But if drinking offers them an opportunity to be with other people and creates a feeling of comradery, they will continue to consume alcohol despite their initial aversion to it.

Other individuals use alcohol as if it were a medication.

Americans believe there is a pill to cure whatever ails them, and they consume vast quantities of drugs in a desperate quest for a feeling of well-being.

Many of the most widely-used pills, such as Valium and Miltown, relieve anxieties and reduce stress. Large numbers of Americans take tranquilizers as a matter of course. Alcohol, however, is the best anxiety-reducing drug available. (Alcohol is being classified here as a drug like any other medication.) Many people use alcohol to find solace from the buffetings of day-to-day life. They are unable to deal with the tensions and frustrations which besiege them without this comforting crutch.

Biofeedback can help these people learn to deal with stress in more positive ways than by dulling their pain with a drug. A person who uses biofeedback learns to manage stress effectively and to reduce it to tolerable levels. Although no one knows how many alcoholics began their compulsive drinking as a method of getting rid of tension, evidence suggests that large numbers of problem drinkers suffer from severe emotional distress. While some of their stress may arise from the very drinking with which they try to comfort themselves, much of the anxiety which torments them results from simple day-to-day living.

Sources of Stress and Anxiety

Many different things in life cause stress and tension. Anything about which a person cares deeply can become a source of stress, including family, job, and peer group.

The closest and deepest emotional bonds which a person forms are found within the family. Family relations, therefore, are often a major source of stress for most people. A person cares enough about his family to become upset by it.

One problem in the family system of this society is that people live in small, exclusive nuclear units. "Family" means mother, father, and children, and everyone else exists somewhere outside this tiny circle. Such a small unit offers limited emotional resources. In societies where extended families are the norm, aunts, uncles, grandparents, cousins, and other relatives may be very intimate members of the group. They give added warmth and affection and serve as a buffer when there is trouble among some of the family members. In a nuclear family, there is no one to help absorb the shock of a disruption in any of the relationships. If the parents die or divorce each other, the children may be left with no one to care for them except people they consider to be outsiders. When the family does remain intact, the very closeness created by such limited relationships often causes friction.

The occupation or career which an individual pursues can offer a great deal of satisfaction and personal reward. Such an important part of life can, however, cause extreme stress and tension as well. In most positions, a person must work extremely hard to remain where he is. If he entertains visions of advancement, he must put forth an even greater effort. A better job usually means a higher income and increased prestige, but to get a promotion, a person must face fierce competition with many other talented, intelligent people.

A third source of pressure is the peer group. Most people care a great deal what others think of them, especially those with whom they associate regularly and regard as their equals. Beginning with adolescence and sometimes even before, peer groups organize themselves into pecking orders of power and prestige. Competition for higher positions on the ladder causes anxiety and tension for those on the lower rungs, and persons at the top must struggle diligently to maintain their places.

Families, work-related situations, and peer groups, then, are all sources of anxiety and tension for most people. Those who are without families, jobs, or peer groups suffer even more deeply from stress caused by the anguish of extreme loneliness, and distressing feelings of worthlessness and lack of accomplishment and purpose.

For awhile, alcohol numbs the pain of anxiety and stress. As a person continues to seek comfort in the bottle, however, the drinking itself begins to cause difficulty, compounding the original problem rather than affording the solace it once did.

Effects of Alcohol

People who abuse alcohol may suffer acutely from stress and anxiety. They are often unable to cope with even normal day-to-day tensions without the support of the bottle.

Because of its chemical nature, alcohol goes quickly to the bloodstream with a minimum amount of processing by other parts of the body. The soothing effects of alcohol are rapid and reliable, and a person who is experiencing anxiety may believe he has discovered a real friend in the bottle. Within seconds after a person takes a drink, there are physiological, behavioral, and psychological changes within him.

A person who has been drinking experiences a pleasant sense of warmth and comfort. He feels wonderfully relaxed, even to the point of being detached and withdrawn from his problems and painful environment. Two physiological effects of alcohol are responsible for this spurious contentment. The drug causes brain wave activity to slow down, especially in the topmost layer of the cortex. When a person has been drinking, an examination of his brain waves reveals a picture of someone who is drowsy and ready to sleep. As brain wave activity lessens, the individual grows more and more relaxed. Meanwhile, blood vessels near the top of the skin dilate. The flow of blood through these areas becomes more rapid, resulting in a feeling of false warmth.

When an individual continues to rely on alcohol to reduce his painful anxiety and relieve his tension, he develops a tolerance for it. He needs more and more of the drug to produce the relaxed, contented feeling for which he is searching. His increased use begins to trouble him, resulting in a need for even more alcohol to relieve his guilt and anxiety about drinking itself. Thus, alcohol abusers become trapped in a vicious circle which causes them to continue to drink in spite of the many disastrous consequences they experience.

Even if the drinker manages to break the cycle temporarily, he probably will return to using alcohol. Unless he finds new ways of dealing with the stress and tension which gave rise to alcohol abuse originally, he will continue to seek comfort in the bottle.

Other Ways of Reducing Stress

An alternative method of reducing tension, then, would offer new hope to the troubled alcoholic. There are several possibilities:

A drinker might use some other chemical to give him the comfort he needs. Several drugs are now on the market which offer the same kind of relief that the drinker finds in alcohol. The problems with this approach, however, are obvious. Even if the alcoholic discovered a substance which successfully reduced his anxiety, substituting one drug for another would leave him no better off than he was when he was drowning in alcohol.

A second possibility is the use of traditional psychotherapy. The alcoholic would examine the underlying causes of his anxiety and thus become better able to handle it. Unfortunately, traditional forms of psychotherapy have been dismally unsuccessful in treating alcoholism.

A third method, behavior modification, offers a new promise of hope to those seeking effective ways to manage anxiety. It is beyond the scope of this chapter to deal with behavior modification in detail, but growing evidence developed over the last ten years suggests that it can be extremely useful in the treatment of alcoholics. Most of the techniques of behavior modification have been used to stop alcohol abuse without examining the problems which led to excessive drinking in the first place. Treating alcoholics who use the drug as a medication to reduce anxiety requires a combination of these techniques and a careful analysis of the problems which make alcohol use seem so attractive.

Learning to Relax

There are two kinds of problems in learning to manage anxiety. First, the individual must develop effective, positive ways of handling stress within himself. Second, he must make changes in his life which will remove some of the sources of stress.

One of the most interesting and effective methods of handling stress and tension involves the use of biofeedback. The individual develops an amazing control over his own body processes. He can relax muscle tension and even warm cold hands, as well as regulating other symptoms of stress. When a person becomes physically relaxed, psychological relaxation usually follows rapidly.

In biofeedback training, an electronic device collects and records information about body functions and processes, and then proceeds to reflect it back to the subject. When a person actually sees the physical results of his tension, he can learn to create a deliberate state of relaxation within his body. Muscle tension, for example, usually accompanies anxiety. A properly placed set of electrodes makes it possible to record tension levels in muscles just below the skin surface and then display the information directly to the subject, creating a biofeedback loop which rapidly teaches control of this usually involuntary function. With training, a person can maintain this kind of physical relaxation without biofeedback equipment even in extremely stressful situations, resulting in an accompanying state of psychological calmness. Eventually, the individual can produce this relaxation response whenever he wishes.

The advantages of such a skill are incalculable. When a person can relax under stressful conditions, he learns to function more effectively in such situations. He no longer needs alcohol to help him through painful times in his life. Now he has an alternative way of reducing his anxiety, and his new method causes none of the disastrous consequences of alcohol abuse.

Additional Behavior Training Techniques

Biofeedback training is an extremely valuable tool for learning to handle inner stress. The second problem involved in reducing anxiety is discovering ways to change or eliminate the things in life which produce stress in the first place. While no one can expect a life free from tension, other forms of behavioral training can help reduce the amount which a person experiences. People respond to an individual in certain ways because of how he behaves. Techniques such as assertion training, role modeling, and effective, active listening can help a person alter his own behavior in ways which often result in changes within his environment. Perhaps a family situation is causing severe stress for an individual. If he learns to be assertive in his behavior, other family members may begin to treat him differently, resulting in a reduction of stress. Such changes are usually beneficial to everyone concerned.

Reducing the causes of stress and learning to control already existing anxiety are two powerful tools for dealing with alcohol abuse. Researchers currently are testing the model described in this chapter, and the preliminary findings are encouraging. Biofeedback and its associated techniques may turn out to be uniquely effective in the treatment of alcohol abuse.

Psychodrama

*Barbara Czescik, M.A., and
Anthony Del Nuovo, M.A.*

Alcoholics are often hostile and withdrawn. They suffer from extreme loneliness and feelings of isolation and usually need help desperately to develop new social roles. Psychodrama offers the alcoholic a vehicle for releasing his pent-up emotions and learning new ways of interacting with others.

Alcoholic rehabilitation centers across the country are discovering that psychodrama is an effective treatment tool. Its method of encouraging immediate emotional involvement through behavioral actions makes it especially good for working with alcohol abusers. Developed originally about 1924 by Jacob Levy Moreno, M.D., in Vienna, Austria, the technique has since helped thousands of people suffering from a crippling inability to develop positive interpersonal relationships. In the United States, psychodrama has been offering new hope for such problems since the 1950s.

A recent report on the use of the technique concluded that psychodrama: 1) enables its participants to discover their spontaneous selves, 2) helps activate the unconscious fantasies, conflicts, and past life experiences of the patient, 3) intensifies the emotions of the patient and reduces intellectualization, 4) helps set realistic goals, 5) develops motivation, 6) promotes problem solving ability, 7) teaches responsibility, 8) provides an atmosphere where a patient may learn by experience, action, and rational thought, 9) develops personal freedom, 10) develops reassurance and insights, 11) trains for family, work, and community roles, 12) releases anger and rage, 13) explores and develops self-concepts, 14) intensifies reality, 15) restores or eliminates old roles as needed, 16) promotes group identification, community spirit, and citizenship, 17) educates and reeducates,

18) develops responses to reduce conflicts, 19) portrays emerging social situations, 20) provides feedback, 21) repairs emotional deprivation, and 22) reduces social isolation.

These encouraging results suggest that psychodrama offers an opportunity for the alcoholic to restructure himself and his perceptions of the world. Both may be at least partially responsible for starting him along the path to excessive drinking in the first place.

What is psychodrama? How and why does it work? What is the process? What does it offer to an alcoholic who is struggling to maintain sobriety and trying diligently to build a new life, gain self-respect, and learn to express anger at himself and the world around him?

The Psychodramatic Method

The psychodramatic method gives an individual a unique opportunity to approach and explore his inner conflicts by enacting them. As in any play, the main character is the *protagonist*. A psychodrama is different, however, in that the conflicts which the protagonist expresses are problems which trouble his own life. Instead of using a script, players communicate real emotions in their own words. The characters who take the roles of loved ones and friends are *auxiliary egos*. The *director* guides the deeply emotional, real-life drama, and all other people who are present become the *audience*. They represent the real world. Each of these roles is a vital part of the psychodramatic process.

Psychodrama helps the individual learn to interact in the real world in new, effective ways. Some of the goals include: 1) clarifying the feelings of the protagonist, 2) facilitating the expression of emotion, 3) becoming aware of behavior, 4) clarifying goals and values, 5) building support for risk taking, and 6) eliciting feedback from fellow group members about the appropriateness of newly-acquired behaviors, feelings, and attitudes.

The psychodrama usually progresses through three stages: the warm-up, the action, and the integration.

During the warm-up, group members establish rapport with each other. Unless they trust each other with their innermost thoughts and feelings, the drama will be a dreary failure. Group members begin by engaging in spontaneous conversation and behavior, and then direct their attention toward some specific idea or task. Finally, they choose a protagonist and begin to explore the problem which besieges him. Auxiliary egos, also selected by the group, help the protagonist to present the special conflict with which he wishes to deal. This begins the action portion of the psychodrama.

The play continues as actors focus on core issues in the conflict, exploring unexpressed emotions, working through resistances, and pointing out communication cues. Finally, there is "act hunger" or "act completion," which often involves a spontaneous burst of strong, utterly sincere emotion, followed by new, more productive behaviors. Instead of intellectualizing his problem, the protagonist grapples directly with it through feelings and action. He becomes much more free about expressing himself and begins to make use of his own spontaneous creativity.

In the integration phase, the protagonist shares the new roles, feelings, and behaviors which he learned from the psychodrama. The whole group participates freely in the discussion. Usually, it is not only the protagonist who becomes emotionally involved in the play. Several audience members or auxiliary egos may have seen clear parallels to their own lives and may wish to share their feelings and reactions with the other group members. The session closes with a look at support-building techniques and reentry into everyday life, a summary of what the group accomplished, planning for the next time, and finally, a discussion about the frightening prospect of leaving the group.

Achieving Role Clarity

Each person plays many roles in life. Different situations require different behaviors. A healthy individual can integrate all of his various roles into one harmonious personality. Sometimes, however, the roles a person plays become confused, resulting in a serious conflict which causes stress and anxiety. In the case of the alcoholic, this tension leads often to the desire for a drink.

One of the primary goals of psychodrama is to reduce role conflict and confusion so that role clarity and satisfaction evolves. During the psychodrama, actors are free to practice role reversals and try out new behaviors. Effective and appropriate responses to old conflicts often blossom spontaneously in this open, creative atmosphere. The process encourages the alcoholic to change his perceptions of both himself and the world.

Another goal of psychodrama is to recreate the spontaneity which alcohol abuse has destroyed. By participating in a psychodrama, an individual develops a new kind of spontaneity which he can use in his recently-discovered feeling and behavioral responses.

Psychodrama offers a unique opportunity to confine and explore the drinking and life-style patterns which have caused such anguish for the alcoholic. Most alcoholics do not really know why they drink, and their destructive habits bewilder and disturb them. Through psychodrama, they can begin to understand themselves better. More importantly, however, the alcoholic sees the disastrous consequences of his drinking and the injurious effects it has on family, social life, economic stability, and employment. The drinker can also examine carefully the situations which have caused him to seek refuge in alcohol. He then rehearses more productive methods of dealing with the same issues, developing new skills which he carries over into real life.

Psychodramatic Techniques

Several specific techniques exist within the total psychodramatic method. Each has a particular purpose, and all of them interact together to make psychodrama a powerful tool for learning new behaviors. A few of the specific techniques which may be helpful include the following:

1. The group chooses an auxiliary ego to personify alcohol. They may call him Alcohol, Booze, The Bottle, or whatever seems appropriate to the protagonist. Often a highly emotional tug-of-war ensues between The Bottle and either the spouse or the inner self of the protagonist. The drama may provoke a new response to this old, troublesome conflict, and the protagonist can practice behavior which results in a satisfying outcome. Other auxiliary egos may integrate the vital role which Alcoholics Anonymous can play in helping to win this battle.

2. An alcoholic must understand the intricate connection between his emotions and his abusive drinking. In this psychodrama, an auxiliary ego plays the role of his hidden feelings, helping him to recognize and clarify suppressed discomfort, hostility, anger, or anxiety. Or the protagonist may take the role of a friend trying to talk another alcoholic out of taking a drink. Such a situation forces the protagonist to face at least his own resistances. Each of these plays encourages self-awareness.

3. A third drama places the alcoholic in social situations where someone is pressuring him to have a drink. How will he respond when a friend makes the familiar and tempting suggestion, "Let's go have a drink"? What will he say when an acquaintance demands, "What do you mean, you don't want to drink?" "What's wrong with you?" The group analyzes his method of answering these difficult questions and explores his conscious and unconscious motivations. An alcoholic who is struggling to maintain his hard-won sobriety will almost

certainly encounter dangerous pressures such as these. The drama prepares him to deal with real situations which may imperil his sobriety.

4. A fourth psychodrama helps the alcoholic with the arduous readjustment process he faces when he returns home after treatment. How does he respond to a family who may be harboring resentment? What does he do when he interviews for a job? Where shall he spend the hours that he used to waste alone in a bar or gulping drinks at home? The alcoholic faces the difficult but exciting challenge of developing new interests and discovering activities he enjoys. He may try out various possibilities onstage, such as new hobbies, attending plays and concerts, or pursuing new people. The psychodrama offers also an opportunity to explore other situations which may lie ahead of him. These may include a new employment opportunity, a successful marriage, or a divorce fraught with as little emotional upheaval as possible. Such plays are called future-dramas, and they help the alcoholic learn to deal with various forms of anxiety which he will have to face as he continues in his new way of life.

In psychodrama, the emotional involvement of an individual is deep and immediate. This gives the method an impact which "talk therapies" do not have. The technique offers unique insights which often lead recovering alcoholics to change dramatically both their perceptions of the world and themselves. They develop a healthy ability to cope with stressful situations, they lose their crippling fears, and they feel more accepted, secure, and have better self-images. Those who participate in psychodrama develop a deep and lasting understanding of other people and their problems, but they are able to separate the difficulties of others from their own lives. They grow less demanding, more tolerant, and have more precious ego strength. The valuable skills they develop help them to be more sociable and less manipulative.

An individual becomes totally involved in psychodrama.

He immerses his body and mind and his whole personality in the action of reality. He begins to understand how marvelous it can feel to be spontaneous and responsible, and to be able to cope productively with stress. He discovers he is able to act freely and without fear. The alcoholic is not just a spectator. He himself creates the action. Perhaps it is for these reasons that psychodrama works so well.

Psychodrama is not only a therapeutic method. It is a powerful educational tool and an excellent role-training instrument as well. The technique is flexible enough to deal effectively with the myriad of problems, situations, and troubled personalities which alcoholics carry with them to the sessions. In some ways, this successful treatment modality may even offer a kind of substitute for alcohol. The problem drinker can express hidden emotions and display suppressed behavior which, in the past, alcohol alone could set free. He learns positive new behaviors as well, and prepares himself for a healthy reentry into the world.

When used in conjunction with the help and support of family members and friends, psychodrama can help the recovering alcoholic develop a completely new frame of reference. From this can come a whole new life.

Power Motivation Training

Richard Boyatzis, Ph.D.

Adapted from *Power Motivation Training: Instructor's Manual*, by R. E. Boyatzis (Boston: McBer and Company, 1975).

The helpless feeling of being powerless troubles everyone from time to time. The problems of life or the inner emotions of a person begin to overwhelm him, leaving him weak and without hope.

There may be times when an individual feels potent and influential, but is still dissatisfied because he wants to be even more powerful. In such a situation, a person may express a desire "to get higher," or "to rise above the occasion," or "to get on top of things."

Feeling powerless reflects a need to restore balance in a particular area of life. A person may be concerned about self-control (power over self), or about prestige or status (power in the eyes of others), or having impact on others (power to influence people and events), or about inner strength (power to be).

Everyone wants to believe he has control over his own life. When various events bring a person face-to-face with the disturbing realization that he cannot regulate the world to his own satisfaction, he experiences the distressing feeling of powerlessness (see Figure 4, page 103). A person may feel he has lost control of himself and his surroundings if he fails to perform up to the standards he has set for himself or those of a group to whom he wishes to be close. Shouldering the burden of a new responsibility, boredom, anticipating failure or rejection, or stressful changes in life may all cause a person to suffer from powerlessness. Even a celebration can lead to a vague feeling of emptiness, causing a person to wonder if he is somehow missing something. He may try desperately "to get higher" or overcome the feeling of being out of control of his life.

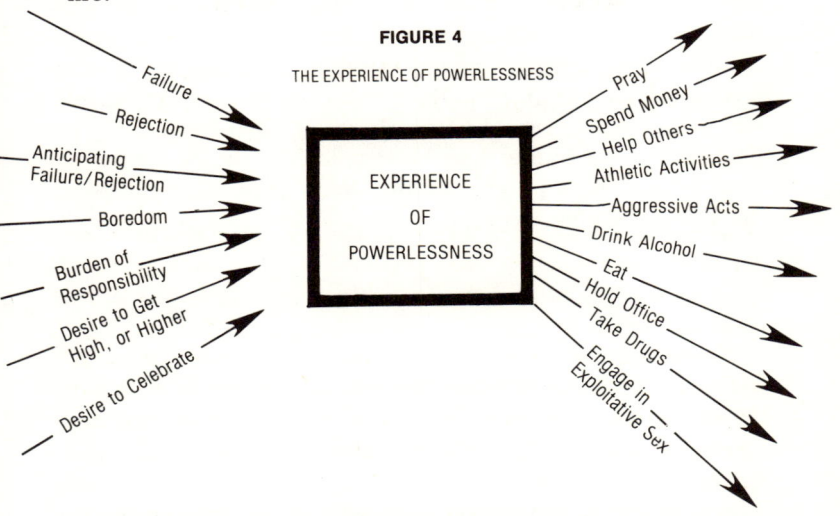

FIGURE 4

THE EXPERIENCE OF POWERLESSNESS

Inputs (leading to experience of powerlessness): Failure, Rejection, Anticipating Failure/Rejection, Boredom, Burden of Responsibility, Desire to Get High, or Higher, Desire to Celebrate

Outputs (responses): Pray, Spend Money, Help Others, Athletic Activities, Aggressive Acts, Drink Alcohol, Eat, Hold Office, Take Drugs, Engage in Exploitative Sex

NOTE: Reprinted from *Power Motivation Training: Instructor's Manual*, by R. E. Boyatzis (Boston: McBer and Company, 1975). © 1975 by McBer and Company.

Some people, however, respond positively to adversity. Failure may stimulate a wish to perform better next time, and rejection may drive a person to work more diligently toward satisfying relationships with others.

The feeling of powerlessness is common to everyone. *Why a person has this unpleasant experience is not nearly so important as how he responds to it.*

When the distressing sensation of powerlessness overwhelms a person, he needs desperately to reestablish balance in his life by succeeding at something. There are many different ways of restoring a feeling of strength (see Figure 4). The particular activities which lead to a feeling of power vary greatly from person to person. Past experiences, cultural differences, and physiological variations, as well as factors outside the control of an individual such as expenses or the stereotypes of society, all influence what will make a certain person feel successful and strong. An individual may pray, for example, seeking power through spiritual or cosmic forces. He may engage in athletics, exploitive sex, or aggressive acts. He may run for office in some organization, try to help others, eat more than he should, or simply spend his money. For some people, taking drugs or drinking alcohol brings a satisfying feeling of power, at least temporarily.

Powerlessness As a Life-Style

When a person repeatedly chooses one activity to help him feel powerful to the exclusion of all others, he risks harmful consequences. Looking for strength in alcohol only, for example, may eventually lead to the same kind of events which caused powerlessness in the first place. When a person uses alcohol as a panacea for all that troubles him, even the anticipation of unpleasant events may send him running for the bottle. This dangerous behavior pattern may lead to alcoholism.

The drinker begins showing up late for work with a hangover. He may escape with such irresponsible behavior for awhile, but eventually, his supervisor will reprove him for his tardiness or loss of productivity. When he returns home after the reprimand, he drinks even more to soothe his ruffled feelings. His wife may wonder why he drinks so much and may begin to nag him about it. Now he feels powerless both at work and at home, and he reaches for the bottle to bolster his sagging ego. As his drinking increases, more and more events happen which make him feel weak and inadequate. Trying desperately to get rid of these distressing emotions, he consumes even more alcohol, falling into a vicious circle in which his entire life-style becomes one of powerlessness (see Figure 5, page 106).

Regardless of what events stimulate this destructive behavior pattern in the first place, the result is psychological and physiological dependence on alcohol. The very fact that a person chooses alcohol habitually to overcome his feelings of weakness indicates a strong psychological dependence. As the cycle continues, the individual loses control of himself and his ability to choose among different ways of reestablishing a feeling of strength. Alcohol gains an unbreakable hold on his whole way of life, rendering him completely helpless against it.

Implications of PMT

A person who relies on alcohol to overcome his feelings of inadequacy falls into a destructive downward spiral of powerlessness. He needs to find new, more productive ways of handling the unpleasant experience of being unable to control completely his life and the world around him. PMT (Power Motivation Training) offers a positive alternative for dealing with his feelings.

Figure 6 (page 107) shows that PMT intervenes in the dynamics of powerlessness in two ways. First, the technique helps the client recognize when disturbing feelings of helplessness are about to overwhelm him. Through various behavioral exercises, verbal discussions, and the development of an Early Warning System, he becomes aware of what makes him feel powerless. Instead of plunging into an abyss of weakness and helplessness, he learns to control successfully his moments of powerlessness (see the left side of Figure 6).

Second, PMT helps the client discover positive ways to feel powerful which do not involve abusing alcohol. During the PMT sessions, he has a unique opportunity to practice several of them (see the right side of Figure 6).

Through exercises and discussions, the client learns how

106 / THE IMPACT OF ALCOHOLISM

FIGURE 5

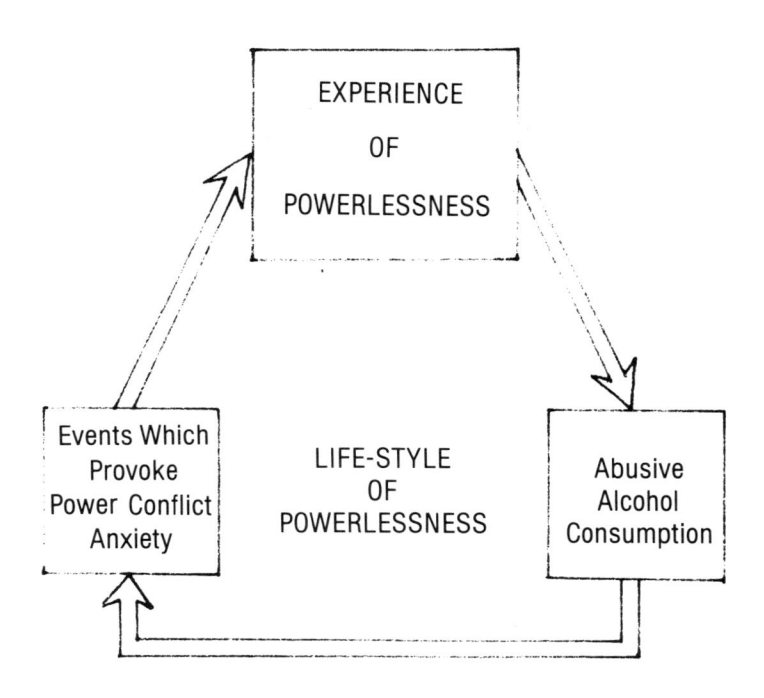

EXPERIENCE OF POWERLESSNESS

Events Which Provoke Power Conflict Anxiety

LIFE-STYLE OF POWERLESSNESS

Abusive Alcohol Consumption

NOTE: Reprinted from *Power Motivation Training: Instructor's Manual*, by R. E. Boyatzis (Boston: McBer and Company, 1975). © 1975 by McBer and Company.

the destructive cycle of powerlessness works and why it is vital that he develop the valuable skills which will allow him to monitor and control his feelings of inadequacy. He learns also how to recognize and use alternatives to alcohol. Armed with this knowledge, as well as the skills and self-awareness he develops in PMT, the client can break the deadly grip of alcohol and build a new life-style (see Figure 7, page 108).

TREATMENT / 107

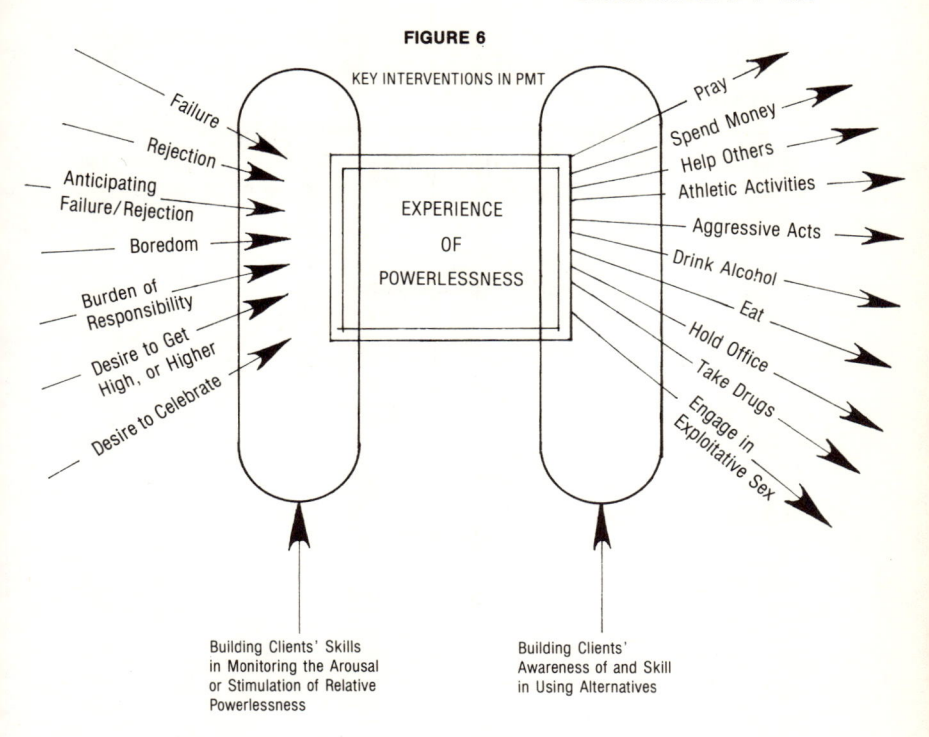

FIGURE 6

KEY INTERVENTIONS IN PMT

Inputs to Experience of Powerlessness:
- Failure
- Rejection
- Anticipating Failure/Rejection
- Boredom
- Burden of Responsibility
- Desire to Get High, or Higher
- Desire to Celebrate

Outputs from Experience of Powerlessness:
- Pray
- Spend Money
- Help Others
- Athletic Activities
- Aggressive Acts
- Drink Alcohol
- Eat
- Hold Office
- Take Drugs
- Engage in Exploitative Sex

Building Clients' Skills in Monitoring the Arousal or Stimulation of Relative Powerlessness

Building Clients' Awareness of and Skill in Using Alternatives

NOTE: Reprinted from *Power Motivation Training: Instructor's Manual*, by R. E. Boyatzis (Boston: McBer and Company, 1975). © 1975 by McBer and Company.

Objectives of PMT

The overall purpose of PMT is to offer people the opportunity to gain knowledge and build skills which will help them to lead satisfying, productive lives, now and in the future. The program guides the client through a four-step process designed to achieve this goal.

First, the program teaches him how his thoughts, fantasies, and feelings relate to his behavior. A delicate interaction exists between his emotions and his drinking, and until he understands how it works, he will be unable to break the vicious cycle of alcohol abuse.

Second, the client must learn to recognize when he begins to feel powerless. When he discovers what triggers his moments of helplessness, he can begin to learn how to control them.

FIGURE 7

BREAKING THE POWER OF ALCOHOL
AND A LIFE-STYLE OF POWERLESSNESS

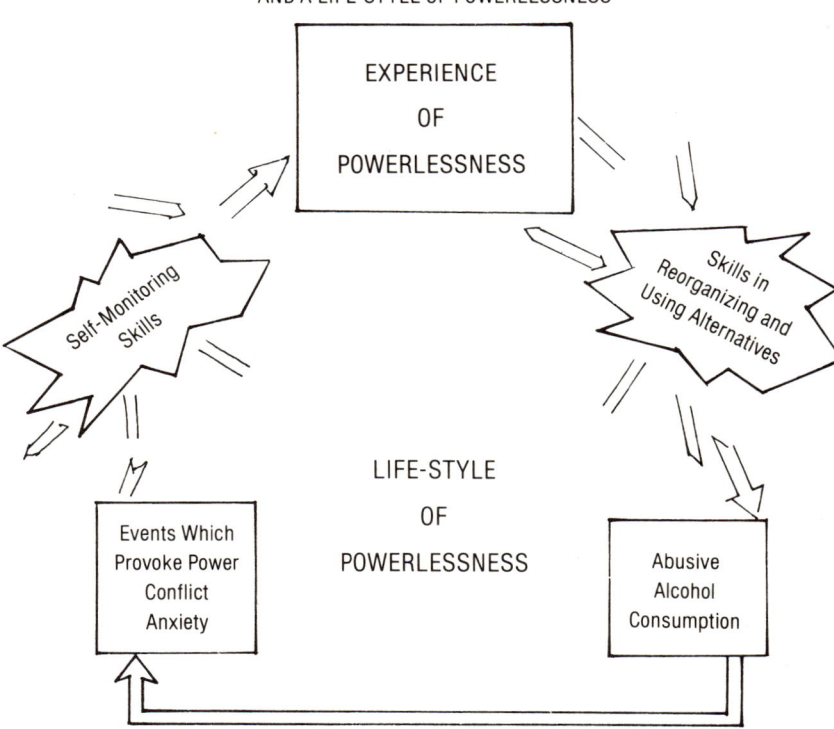

```
                    EXPERIENCE
                        OF
                    POWERLESSNESS

   Self-Monitoring                    Skills in
       Skills                      Reorganizing and
                                   Using Alternatives

                    LIFE-STYLE
                        OF
   Events Which     POWERLESSNESS      Abusive
   Provoke Power                       Alcohol
     Conflict                        Consumption
     Anxiety
```

NOTE: Reprinted from *Power Motivation Training: Instructor's Manual*, by R. E. Boyatzis (Boston: McBer and Company, 1975). © 1975 by McBer and Company.

Third, he needs to learn other ways to feel powerful besides abusing alcohol. Then, when he begins to feel weak and inadequate, there will be several things he can do to correct the situation.

Fourth, the client has an opportunity to put his new solutions into practice so that when he chooses one during a real-life situation, he knows it will work.

By the end of training, the client should be able to: 1) state how thoughts and feelings about power lead him into the trap of drinking behavior, 2) use his "Early Warning System" to identify moments when powerlessness begins to overwhelm him, 3) list several things he can do at such times to make himself feel powerful, 4) use his new skills to deal effectively with arguments, conflicts, pressures, and boredom which made him feel powerless, and 5) describe specific plans for future growth and development.

If the client achieves these goals, he will be able to build a life-style free from alcohol. Guiding him through these four important steps is no easy task. In order to be effective, the program must: a) provide the client with a conceptual framework which will help him understand his drinking behavior, b) teach new skills in self-awareness (these exercises include the development of the "Early Warning System), c) offer a safe, nonthreatening environment in which the client can experiment with his skills, and d) provide actual experiences in which he practices his new behavior.

The program involves about thirty hours of small group sessions. Ten units of three hours each usually offer the most effective framework for developing this important growth experience.

Objective I:

Connecting Drinking Behavior to Power Concerns

Unless a person understands how his feelings of weakness lead him into drinking behavior, he will not be able to break the destructive cycle of alcohol abuse. To accomplish this important goal, the individual must examine himself carefully, and in order to do this successfully, he must feel comfortable. His environment must be safe and nonthreatening. A deep commitment to this difficult process of self-examination is imperative, because the individual must relinquish his old beliefs about *how* and *why* he acts as he does.

The early units should encourage the client to open himself up to self-examination and introduce him to the basic concepts of the program. Clients usually suffer from painful ambivalence about receiving help. Short behavioral exercises can put them at ease and create a nonthreatening mood, as well as encourage self-examination. Arm wrestling, for example, can be a good way to get the group to interact with each other and to begin the delicate process of self-observation during a power conflict. Another possibility might be role playing a family conflict involving a recovering alcoholic, his wife, and their two children. This exercise gives the group members a chance to examine objectively an experience which is a common occurrence for many of them.

Alcoholics are skilled at creating sophisticated explanations for their drinking behavior. They weave intricate stories to hide it or justify it to themselves and others. During PMT, the client learns to recognize this prevaricating behavior as a vain attempt to avoid the painful feelings of weakness and inadequacy which follow his drinking episodes. He begins also to understand how painful sensations of powerlessness relate to the obsessive desire to drink, and why these feelings arise from conflict situations which he examined earlier.

Objective II:
Developing an Early Warning System

A person cannot hope to control his distressing feelings of weakness and inadequacy unless he learns to recognize them before they overwhelm him completely. Developing an Early Warning System helps him to do this. This system is easy to remember and use, so he can call upon it even during moments of stress. Exercises and diagnostic questionnaires make the client aware of what kinds of situations cause him to feel powerless, and a special checklist of adjectives helps him to describe his different moods. He analyzes his innermost thoughts for themes of power and begins to recognize "power plays" in his behavior. Throughout the remainder of the program, the counselor encourages the client to monitor carefully his moods and fantasies.

The Early Warning System is the key to developing conscious control of feelings of powerlessness and inadequacy. With the new awareness which the Early Warning System offers, the client is no longer a slave to alcohol. He is free to choose an alternative way of making himself feel good before powerlessness overcomes him.

Objectives III, IV, and V: Practicing and Planning Alternative Behavior

Unless an individual discovers an alternative to drinking which affords him just as much satisfaction as alcohol, he is almost certain to return to the bottle. The new behavior must also be easy for him.

During the later sessions of PMT, the client has a unique opportunity to try out and practice different activities which make him feel successful and powerful. He completes a personal list of options which work for him, but during the process, several activities receive emphasis, including relaxation techniques, physical fitness exercises, athletics, helping others, and developing more effective methods of influencing people. Other possibilities might be counseling, writing, hobbies and crafts, earning money, self study, and prayer.

Relaxation exercises receive special attention because clients often need help in dealing with stress and anxiety. The program may include a simple form of yoga and meditation training. As the client practices muscle relaxation, special breathing, and mental detachment, the control he has over himself increases surprisingly.

Interpersonal relationships are another important area in which most clients have experienced difficulties. The individual may suffer grave doubts about his ability to relate to others. Role playing can help him to develop effective strategies for influencing people without manipulating them. He learns to recognize goals, to share the risk of resolving a conflict, and to end by making everyone involved feel powerful and good about himself.

The final stages of the program involve real-life situations in which the client can practice his new interpersonal and self-examination skills. He may discuss old conflicts and threatening situations with family and friends. One client, for example, talked about the PMT material with his wife, and together they developed an Early Warning System, agreeing to sit calmly and discuss any issue which set the system off.

Unrealistic aspirations continually plague alcoholics. Through PMT, a client learns to recognize that many of his goals involve a discouragingly high risk of failure. He can then discuss the effects of such behavior on family life, work, recreational activities, driving, and his compulsive desire to drink.

During the last two sessions, the client shifts from setting short-term daily goals, which allow him to see immediate success, to planning long-range goals. He learns that seeking aid from others does not mean he is too weak to help himself, but is simply a way of using available resources. He sets goals for personal change which will make it possible for him to test his progress. Many clients find it important to include ways to maintain sobriety and continuing treatment in their future plans.

CHAPTER VIII

Attitude and Behavior Changes

Steven F. Bucky, Ph.D.

When an alcoholic goes into treatment, he undertakes a long and arduous process which, if it is successful, will create for him a whole new kind of life. He needs all the help and support he can get during this difficult period. Friends and relatives who have erroneous beliefs and attitudes about his disease add to his burden. If a loved one is to offer real support and help, he or she must have correct information. Here are some common statements about alcoholism, along with the facts about each one.

1. "The alcoholic enjoys getting drunk."

    Fact: Alcoholism causes great personal anguish and has devastating effects on physical and emotional well-being, interpersonal relationships, and work performance.

2. "Anyone who is alcoholic simply lacks willpower."

    Fact: Alcoholism is a progressive disease which requires treatment. It has little to do with willpower.

3. "Alcohol abuse allows the individual to escape from reality."

   Fact: A person who has reached the Chronic Stage of alcoholism is no longer capable of perceiving reality accurately, so he has no need to escape from it.

4. "If the alcoholic can stop drinking for any length of time, he does not have an alcohol problem."

   Fact: Many alcoholics can stop drinking for days, weeks, or even months. Inevitably, however, they are drawn back into the downward spiral of alcohol abuse.

5. "Alcoholics are derelicts."

   Fact: Recent statistics indicate that only about 3 to 5 percent of alcoholics are on skid row. Most of them have jobs and families.

6. "Beer and light wine are unlikely to cause alcohol-related difficulties."

   Fact: Alcohol is alcohol. The form in which it comes makes no difference. A person can become alcoholic from drinking beer as easily as he can from whiskey.

7. "Alcoholism can be inherited."

   Fact: At the present time, the question of a genetic predisposition toward alcohol remains uncertain. The only thing that is sure is that a person needs to drink excessively to become alcoholic.

8. "Alcoholics are highly sociable."

   Fact: Heavy drinkers usually withdraw from other people. They have trouble maintaining meaningful interpersonal relationships and tend to isolate themselves both at home and at work.

9. "Alcoholism can be cured."

   Fact: Alcoholism is a chronic illness for which there is no known cure. The most effective form of treatment is membership in Alcoholics Anonymous, which helps the individual to deal with his problem one day at a time. Members of AA do not refer to themselves as "cured." They are "recovering alcoholics."

10. "Coffee helps a person become sober"

    Fact: Coffee has no effect on the rate at which the body metabolizes alcohol.

11. "Alcoholism is a moral issue."

    Fact: Alcoholism is a disease, and has no more to do with morals and ethics than diabetes or cancer.

Changing Attitudes and Behavior

The alcoholic himself must make changes in his behavior and attitudes. Here are some things he must do as he continues on the path to contented sobriety:

1. Maintain a neat physical appearance. When a person looks good, he usually feels good about himself. The alcoholic should make a real effort to practice good grooming habits.

2. Eat properly. Alcoholics are usually undernourished and develop distressing symptoms of malnutrition. Regular, well-balanced meals are a vital part of treatment.

3. Overcome denial. Denial is a favorite defense mechanism of alcoholics for avoiding anxiety and pain. Until a person learns to see himself and life realistically, he cannot hope for recovery.

4. Express anger openly. Alcoholics often turn their hostile feelings inward until they explode in a sudden outburst of anger. An individual must learn positive ways to express these volatile emotions.
5. Deal with anxiety. High anxiety levels often are at least partially responsible for excessive drinking. Alcoholics should engage in activities which help to reduce these feelings, such as athletics, running or walking, and other forms of physical exercise.
6. Develop effective interpersonal relationships. Alcoholics frequently have difficulty maintaining close relationships with others. They must begin discovering new and positive ways of relating to people. For awhile, it may be necessary to avoid old drinking buddies.
7. Be able to refuse a drink comfortably. An alcoholic must learn to ask for a soft drink as easily as he once accepted a martini.

Suggestions for the Family

Family members suffer deeply from the myriad of destructive problems which have invaded their home. The spouse bears the heaviest burden. The following suggestions may help her to deal more effectively with the difficulties which face her:

1. Try to remain calm and unemotional.
2. Learn the facts about alcoholism.
3. Talk with others who are familiar with alcoholism.
4. Get treatment for yourself. An alcoholic will frequently follow the lead of his spouse and get into treatment himself.
5. Try to include the alcoholic in family activities.
6. Be open with children about the drinking problem.
7. Encourage new interests in all family members.
8. Be patient.

ATTITUDE AND BEHAVIOR CHANGES / 117

9. Do not try to punish the alcoholic for his drinking.
10. Do not make excuses for his drinking.
11. Do not feel responsible.
12. Refuse to ride with the alcoholic when he has been drinking.
13. Do not hide liquor bottles.
14. Do not argue with him when he is drunk.
15. Do not feel it is necessary to drink with him.
16. Do not feel guilty.

All these suggestions do not apply to every family in which there is a drinking problem. Most people who live with an alcoholic, however, will recognize changes they can make to improve their own situations.

Recovery from the destructive disease of alcoholism is a life-long process requiring a whole new way of life. There are no magic cures, and progress is often slow and discouraging. The rewards, however, are well worth the struggle. Inner peace and contentment, normal family life, and restored physical and mental health are all part of a new life free from alcohol.

Summary

Alcohol abuse and alcoholism have a dramatic effect on the physical, psychological, emotional, and interpersonal wellbeing of the abuser and all of the people with whom he/she comes into contact. Alcoholism develops slowly. It is an insidious process that, unfortunately, goes unnoticed for many years. The individual who drinks heavily tends to deny that a drinking problem exists. Significant others ignore the problem or help the individual to cover up, and as a result, help naively to prolong the agony for all concerned.

Alcoholism can be treated. The most effective form of treatment at the present time is Alcoholics Anonymous (AA). The other forms of treatment described in this volume are viewed as additional therapeutic modalities for many individuals suffering from alcoholism. Early detection and prompt treatment are necessary prerequisites to a successful reduction of the impact that alcohol abuse and alcoholism have on the individual, the family, industry, our legal system, and society as a whole.

Notes

I. *Signs and Symptoms*

1 E. M. Jellinek, *The Disease Concept of Alcoholism* (New Haven, CT: College and University Press; New Brunswick, NJ: Hillhouse Press, 1960), pp. 33-149.
2 D. Cahalan, *Problem Drinkers* (San Francisco: Jossey Bass, 1970), pp. 26-27.

IV. *Legal Aspects of Alcoholism*

1 *Alcohol Education Program*, Fact Sheet 2 (Tulsa, OK: Operation Threshold, 1973), pp. 1-3.

V. *Interpersonal Effects of Alcohol Abuse*

1 J. J. Strack and L. A. Dutton, "Spouse Involvement in the Treatment of Alcoholism," *Insight* 17 (1971), p. 3.
2 S. Wilsnak, "The Impact of Sex Roles on Women's Alcohol Use and Abuse," *Alcoholism Problems in Women and Children*, ed. M. Greenblatt and M. Schuckit (New York: Grune and Stratton, 1976), pp. 37-64.

VI. *Effects of Alcohol Abuse on Work Performance*

1 *A Company Program on Alcoholism*, 5th ed. rev. (New York: Christopher D. Smithers Foundation, 1974), p. 13.
2 *Ibid.*, p. 17.
3 *The Key Role of Labor in Employee Alcoholism Programs*, 4th ed. rev. (New York: Christopher D. Smithers Foundation, 1974), p. 4.
4 E. M. Jellinek, *The Disease Concept of Alcoholism* (New Haven, CT: College and University Press; New Brunswick, NJ: Hillhouse Press, 1960), pp. 33-149.

VII. *Treatment*

1 *Alcoholics Anonymous Preamble* (Card) (New York: Alcoholics Anonymous World Services).
2 *Alcoholics Anonymous*, 3rd ed. rev. (New York: Alcoholics Anonymous World Services, 1976), pp. 59-60.

3 *Twelve Steps and Twelve Traditions* (New York: Alcoholics Anonymous World Services), p. 63.
4 *Ibid.*, p. 77.
5 *Alcoholics Anonymous*, p. 83.
6 *Ibid.*, p. 103.
7 *Ibid.*, p. 564.
8 J. L. Kellermann, *Guide for the Family of the Alcoholic* (Center City, MN: Hazelden, 1973), pp. 11-12.

Works Cited

1. *Alcohol Education Program*. Fact Sheet 2. Tulsa, OK: Operation Threshold, 1973.
2. *Alcoholics Anonymous*. 3rd ed. rev. New York: Alcoholics Anonymous World Services, 1976.
3. *Alcoholics Anonymous Preamble* (Card). New York: Alcoholics Anonymous World Services.
4. Boyatzis, R. E. *Power Motivation Training: Instructor's Manual*. Boston: McBer and Company, 1975.
5. Cahalan, D. *Problem Drinkers*. San Francisco: Jossey Bass, 1970.
6. *A Company Program on Alcoholism*. 8th ed. rev. New York: Christopher D. Smithers Foundation, 1974.
7. *First Special Report to the U.S. Congress on Alcohol and Health*. Publication 74-68. Rockville, MD: Department of Health, Education, and Welfare, 1971.
8. Jellinek. E. M. *The Disease Concept of Alcoholism*. New Haven, CT: College and University Press; New Brunswick, NJ: Hillhouse Press, 1960.
9. Kellermann, J. L. *Guide for the Family of the Alcoholic*. Center City, MN: Hazelden Books, 1973.
10. *The Key Role of Labor in Employee Alcoholism Programs*. 4th ed. rev. New York: Christopher D. Smithers Foundation, 1974.
11. Strack, J. J. and Dutton, L. A. "Spouse Involvement in the Treatment of Alcoholism." *Insight* 17 (1971): 3.
12. *Twelve Steps and Twelve Traditions*. New York: Alcoholics Anonymous World Services, 1952.
13. Wilsnak, S. "The Impact of Sex Roles on Women's Alcohol Use and Abuse." *Alcoholism Problems in Women and Children*. Edited by M. Greenblatt and M. Schuckit. New York: Grune and Stratton, 1976.